ONTOLOGICAL AND ETHICAL FOUNDATIONS OF LAW

Ontological and Ethical Foundations of Law

Javier de Pedro

Spring Publications Limited

Contents

First Printing, 2022

ISBN 978-988-75983-2-9

This edition published in 2021 by Spring Publications
Spring Publications Limited
www.spring-books.com
info@spring-books.com

1

An Introduction to Rights and Duties

1.1 Historical Perspective

At the end of Second World War, mankind witnessed an unprecedented event of profound consequences. The winning Allies—the United States, the United Kingdom, the Soviet Union and the like—constituted themselves as judges of the leaders of the defeated nations—Germany, Italy, Japan—, brought them to court and punished them as responsible for the crimes they had committed against humanity, as war criminals.

In those days ABC, a Madrid newspaper, published together in the front page two pictures: one of a Russian accusing one of the Nazi leaders, the other one a reproduction of one of the most famous paintings of Velazquez, the *Surrender of Breda,* depicting the surrender of that city in the Low Countries to the Spanish infantry[1].

The conquered city was seen in the background, laying on a gentle hill, across a forest of lances; the winner of the day, Ambrogio Spinola, receiving the keys of the city from the defeated leader, Maurice of Nassau, while courteously embracing him. Two different ways of understanding war.

It was often understood among pagans that war was not about rights or wrongs, but about sheer power. The winner simply liquidated his enemies, or made them his slaves after raping their women and plundering their cities. It was the law of the strongest, Darwin's survival of the fittest. There is no mercy for the conquered people![2]

War has always been cruel but, at least in theory, Christianity has tried to civilize the outcome of human conflicts. In history, real Christian men fought because they could find no better way of solving problem of conflicting rights. None of them doubted that: a) men possessed real rights; b) conflicts of rights were unavoidable given human limitations; and c) men were entitled to defend their rights. Once the case was solved and justice reestablished, men could be friends again. *Opus justitiae, pax:* Peace was the work of justice.

In Nuremberg, the defeated were condemned to death; was that legal action morally justifiable, or was it the biggest parody of justice ever seen? Because some among those condemning the Nazi leaders were responsible for crimes as great as those committed by the accused. It looked like a modern version of the *Vae victis*!—woe the vanquished!

Probably it was not strictly like that. Certainly, the defeated were tried in a Court that was not an independent body, possessed no jurisdiction, and considered crimes against laws never promulgated; besides some among the winners had also committed unspeakable crimes against humanity: the purges of Stalin, the atomic bomb over Hiroshima and Nagasaki, and the bombing of Dresden, just to mention a few. Altogether, it looked like vengeance rather than justice.

Yet. there was a kind of consensus among upright men that the Nazis had been the unjust aggressors: therefore, there was some sort of fundamental justice that had to be redressed, even if the procedures were not justified, and will never be justified before the Courts of History.

Soon after the War, a group of men of good will worked towards the promulgation of a code of fundamental human rights, that crystallized into the Charter of the United Nations and the Universal Declaration of Human Rights (1948). They were mostly men coming from the Christian tradition. They were in agreement with that intuition of the ancient Greeks that freedom is something natural to man and must be protected by just laws; they were also well acquainted with the tradition of Roman Law that granted to the citizens superb positive rights; they were familiar as well with the Christian concept of man, created in the image and likeness of God; they were also aware of the long, unique elaboration of canonical law, always inspired by the *salus animarum.* And, finally, they wholehearted subscribed to that astonishing philosophical and juridical construction known as the *ius gentium* (i.e., the laws of the nations): a statue of the Dominican Francisco de Vitoria, the father of Christian *ius naturalism,* still graces the gardens of the United Nations in New York.

Human customs had been purified, perfected and made into laws by a long process of rational and theological reflection, and the daily experience of the application of laws that the nations had "given to themselves had effectively contributed to their progressive development. These laws were practical, rational dispositions seeking the common good, and were sanctioned by those who were in charge of the community.

As any other human creation, the laws were not perfect; therefore, when there was a conflict between legal and natural justice, *epikeia*[3] prevailed over the positive laws of the nations. Although in a very stable world laws were part of the traditions of the nation, and therefore, could easily be absorbed by daily human behavior, they were nevertheless changeable and the peoples sent their representatives to the assemblies convened to reconsider them whenever deemed necessary. The King, an independent power at the summit of society, was the supreme judge; but ordinary legal affairs were considered by judges, who were independent men of prudence, versed in the laws of the land, who decided on the conflicts according to principles of justice, law, privilege, and custom; they contributed by their decisions to the progress of the commonwealth of law.

1.2 Leaks in the Foundations

All of a sudden this magnificent edifice started to crumble in the XIX century. It was as if a creek was running through its foundations, threatening its solidity. In reality it had been there for quite some time, maybe since XVII century empiricism[4] questioned the capacity of the human intelligence to reach the nature of things.

Later on, in this series of lectures we will consider the different factors that have historically contributed to undermined that magnificent legal structure. Since we have already reached the last consequences of that process of decay, it is sufficient for now to ask ourselves what has remained of it all. The answer is: almost nothing—a fictitious legal framework that has nowhere to stand on. When Archimedes[5] asked for a fulcrum on which to lean to move the universe, he was implying that having none will demand that everything will be either sheer stillness or sheer movement. The legal universe has followed in our times the later path, that of change, unable to stand on any sure principle.

Today's accepted doctrine is that the legal system of a nation owes nothing to anyone but itself and it should be completely unrelated to any ethical consideration; laws are self-justified, if they have been established following accepted procedures. They need no further foundation except the careful construing and acceptance of the legal procedures. The legal system is therefore conceived as a self-contained universe floating in empty space. There is no fulcrum, no basis in the reality of things for it; but this legal system is self-sufficient and dynamic, since it is endowed with immanent motion. References to anything outside the system must be totally severed, especially those linking it to human nature, God, and the moral order. The justification for such a radical position is not necessarily the denial of God, human nature, or the moral order, but the plural character of contemporary societies.

Jacques Maritain[6], a Frenchman who went from total agnosticism to a deep Christian commitment, one of the best contemporary philosophical minds, a man who left a very profound mark in Christian social thought and in the renewal of metaphysics[7] understood, perhaps better than many, how deep the problem was.

Married to a Russian Jew, a convert to the Catholic faith like himself, he saw the Nazi hordes coming and, fearful for his dear wife's life, he left France, *malgré lui*, for the United States of America. There he found the wholesome American society of the forties, made up of a majority of church-goers, Protestants, Catholics, and Jews, and of a minority of non-believers, all of them living in peace together, in contrast with the horrors of his beloved Europe. He reflected on how that could be possible, since there was no consensus about natural law; he concluded that, at least, there was respect for the rules of the democratic game: the only type of consensus possible in a pluralistic society. Years later, contemplating the ethical collapse of American society and of the West at large, he would disagree with himself.

Meanwhile, his thought left a deep mark in the European Christian-Democratic parties, and even in high ecclesiastical environments. Those holding the reigns of many Western societies, the heirs of the Enlightenment, the believers of ethical Rationalism, applauded the decision of those backward Catholics to jump into the wagon they had always proposed as the only alternative and had fought for, either through the ballot or with bullets.

The reality was a little more complex. True Christian people were not willing to renounce to the convictions based on faith and reason that had built Western civilization; but they thought that, for the sake of peace and harmonious coexistence, they should give up their demand that the legal system should be founded on natural morality and fight with democratic means for what they were convinced was right: using the only weapons of majority vote, propaganda, and practical reasons. In other words, they accepted the challenge of renouncing, tactically only, to the most fundamental human notions of what is right and wrong.

In his old age, Maritain ruminated his pessimistic vision of the outcome of such tactical move in the soliloquies that he collected in his *Le paysant de la Garone* little by little, for a great portion of Christian men and women, the tactical withdrawal had ended up in a total surrender to the enemy. It was as if they were consenting, stone after stone, to the demolition of an old gothic cathedral.

1.3 Legal and Real Rights

The crux of the matter is up to what point it is possible to build up a true human society exclusively founded on legal rights. Our position is that such **human society will only function properly when legal rights are solidly based on real human rights**.

The newspapers recently carried the story of an American lady who had bought a business class plane ticket for her 300 pounds pig, which he calls "my greatest friend," and which she assures "to behave better than most of the people here." It does not look that there is anything intrinsically wrong in granting the pig the right to travel in business class, as long as it is truly well behaved.

A few days ago, I finished reading a book that proposes granting legal personality to lakes, rivers, and the like, as long as they are entitled to have a guardian who can claim their rights. Legal experts could, perhaps, worry about these issues, but this is not the kind of problem we intend to contemplate here.

What really matters is that the pig is under the care of a real lady and has been trained to behave like humans do; and that the guardians of lakes and rivers are human beings or corporations made of human beings.

The issue at the stake is if there is something in humans that entitles them to have rights for the sake of being humans, unlike pigs, lakes, and forests that can possess legal rights only because they behave like humans, are dear to humans, or can be guarded by humans.

Law is unthinkable in a world without men and we do not know of any human society without some form of law or at least of custom, that prevails over the individual will in certain instances. In an animal universe where instinct, adaptability, power, and fitness to survive prevail, human law is unthinkable: what governs an animal group is called the law of the jungle. There are no records of animal societies where collective behavior has been modified by rational discourse and mutual agreements. Legal rights can be attributed to corporations, animals, lakes, and ships, but only human beings can make such attribution, and only human beings can claim the right to something.

There must be an explanation to this different behavior, that sets the bottom line of the distinction between human beings and animals in relation to law: classical thought has called it **rationality**.

Aristotle, a biologist by training and an accurate observer of nature described man as a **rational animal** and what sets man apart from other animals is precisely being endowed with the power of reason.

Not only these rational animals are capable of claiming rights for other creatures, but also they are the only animals who can claim to possess rights for what they are. The process followed by this claim has often been winding and prolonged in time. In olden times the slave girls of Odysseus had no rights; just a century and a half ago, the Negroes in the United States had no rights; but they all eventually got rights because a more Christian, or simply a more civilized society, returned those rights to them on the grounds that they also were human beings. It is significant that those who denied those rights to girls, children, and slaves did so on the assumption that they were not full human beings. Likewise, those who today deny rights to the human fetus try to justify their position on similar grounds.

We can safely conclude that only human beings possess natural rights, while non-humans possess those legal rights that the humans who are in a position to do so decide to grant them.

As for what a man is and for the proper answer to those who historically have played the trick of denying some humans the condition of being fully human and therefore, of being bearers of rights, these are issues to be tackled later in this series.

1.4 Rights and Duties

As soon as a young human creature reaches the age of discernment, he or she discovers that he or she must do what is right and avoid what is wrong. Besides being capable of speaking, laughing, thinking, organizing himself or herself in a society, a human being is radically an ethical animal, because confronted with a variety of possible courses of action, he or she chooses one of them, not only in terms of practicality or self-gratification, but also under the light of a prudential judgement that he or she passes on the right or the wrong of that course of action.

Other people's actions that respect my status in the family, my life and the integrity of my body, my legitimate dominion over things, my good reputation and so on and so forth, are right towards me; otherwise, they are wrong. Status, life, integrity, property, and good name belong to me; they are my rights. Since they are other people's right, too, I owe them to others: it is my duty—it is due to them—that I respect their rights. None of these things depend on the existing laws or customs; they depend only on our being human beings.

A man is call just when he is firmly determined to give always to others what is due to them. Placed in front of a variety of possible courses of action, he discerns what is right from what is wrong, but even when his judgement is correct, he will act justly only if he freely decides to do what is right.

This ethical decision does not depend on any social convention. Surprisingly, in broad lines all men agree to the fundamentals of right and wrong, even if they differ in a number of points, including in understanding what man is. Therefore, notions like justice, rights and duties, primarily correspond to the ethical dimension of man they belong naturally to him. This is why we designate them as **natural rights and duties** and can speak about **naturally just or unjust human actions**.

When a human society recognizes those natural human rights in the laws that it gives to itself, it is acknowledged to be a just society; otherwise, it is unjust. The fulcrum that supports the legal order is natural ethics: that set of fundamental moral precepts that constitute the so-called **natural law**. Without it, a legal system is flawed.

Even if the laws persecuting the Jews in Nazi Germany were perfect from the point of view of legal technicalities, they were ethically unjust laws, and it was men's moral obligation not to obey them.

Notes

[1] Breda fell to Spinola in 1625

[2] *Vae victis*! Proverbial cry of the Gallic King, Brennus, on capturing Rome in 390 BC (Livy).

[3] Legal and moral principle for the application of a law to a particular case, by which the presumed mind of the law-giver and the spirit of the law are to be followed rather than the letter of the law, whenever a conflict between the two arises.

[4] The theory that knowledge is only possible through experience, particularly sense experience.

[5] "Give me but one firm spot on which to stand, and I will move the earth." Archimedes c.287-212 BC.

[6] French philosopher (1882-1973). He became a Catholic in 1906.

[7] Metaphysics is the body of philosophical though that seeks the ultimate reasons of reality. It is also known as Ontology (the science of being). The tide of this lecture series "Ontological Foundations of Law" tells us therefore about the endeavor to explore the ultimate reasons on which Law, any legal system, is to be based. Metaphysics has not been in intellectual fashion for some centuries now, for the simple reason that most thinkers after Descartes (1596-1650) have chosen an immanent position, which establishes the intellectual impossibility of showing that the world at large is independent from the mind perceiving or knowing it. Obviously anyone who has renounced to the objective reality of things, has no use for metaphysics.

2

Person and Law

2.1 Justice as the Result of Orderly Interpersonal Relations

After reflecting upon right and wrong as something that sprouts from our being human, we may ask ourselves about the immediate consequences of right and wrong human behavior. The classical thinkers had simple, clear minds that read in the open book of reality. Plato said that a notion had been handed down up to his times through a long, immemorial tradition: the notion that **each man is to be given what is due to him**. A man ready to give others what is due to them is called a just man; his firm commitment to do it habitually is called the **virtue of justice**. This ethical disposition is considered to be so important that, even if to be good is much more than to be just, a man who is just is ordinarily considered to be a good man.

Certainly, there is a long tradition behind this concept; it is so old that, as far as we know, it goes back to the origin of mankind itself, because it is implicit in one of the simplest expressions of man's rationality: "This is mine. " It can be affirmed without doubt that Western civilization has been built upon the conviction that certain things are due to each man for the sake of being a man and that other men ought to give them to him, because they belong to him. Holy Scripture deals extensively with the just man. Other civilizations, too, are built on such a conviction: otherwise, they would not be civilizations.

When justice is lived, peace reigns in the relations among men. **Opus justitiae, pax**: peace is the fruit of justice. And what is peace? Again, classical wisdom stated that peace is the tranquility of order. This tranquility is enjoyed rather than noticed. On the other hand, the fruit of disorder is unhappiness. When an unwanted disorder is violently or cunningly introduced in a situation of bliss, its disruptive activity is easier to perceive than the peace that characterized the previous state.

That is why Aristotle commented that "the experience of many different forms of injustice makes quite obvious the existence of a variety of forms of justice." And Kant stated that "men's greatest and more frequent troubles are not so much the result of adversity as the fruit of the injustices inflicted upon them by other men."[1] This is plain, common wisdom. What is proper to ethics is precisely to consider the right and wrong in interpersonal relations, given that we acknowledge that, within nature, a person is a being radically different from any other known being.

2.2 Persons

A purely descriptive approach to the behavior of a person, as opposed to that of animals—the other beings which are closer to man—will suffice for the purpose of establishing a departure point between two different concepts of human law. In ordinary language we clearly distinguish between a WHO and a WHAT. When we ask *who did this?*, we expect that someone will respond assuming full responsibility for it: *I did it*; something that we never expect when we ask *what did it?* So, **persons are responsible**, that is to say, they can **answer by themselves**.

Persons give an answer for their actions since they know that their root cause is found within themselves; they are aware of not being determined by compulsive forces beyond their own control, of enjoying a broad level of **freedom of choice**.

Certainly, we humans are not totally free. We have the experience of the inevitability of physical laws and of the complex influences of purely biological tendencies. We are subject to necessity and contingency, but also endowed with that **capacity for self-determination** that makes us to be protagonists of history and builders of technology and culture.

We can choose ends and means because we have the power of foreseeing the future results of our actions and of discerning among the multiple paths leading to them: **we act intentionally**, with a purpose in mind.

Most remarkably, we are capable of holding our own immanence-of enclosing ourselves-and of opening up at will to other personal beings, establishing with them **relations of mutual knowledge, love, and cooperation**: these relations are the result of choice, not of necessity.

We, being free, can communicate the information that we have received, but we may choose instead to send false information to the others; we may respect the legitimate possession of their things, but we may also try to appropriate those things for ourselves, for the sake of our own pleasure or convenience. We may look for the good of the others or look for our own good, even if we are aware that in so doing we inflict harm on them.

Our ability to establish interpersonal relations that either respect or disregard what is due to others is the reason why we, human persons, are **ethical beings.** Even when we attribute an ethical value to our behavior in relation to other natural realities—animals, plants, forests—we base it on the relationship of these realities with other human beings.

As soon as a child reaches the age of reason-that is to say as soon as he or she has acquired that degree of maturity that allows be aware of his or her own identity as a person—the child perceives in his or her heart to be obliged to do to others what is right and avoid what is wrong, while expecting also to be treated by others in the right way, in fairness, and in truth.

This moral sense comes to a human being together with his capacity to deliberate: to consider, for example, whether to pull his sister's hair in order to make her cry, or to tell a lie to his mother is right or wrong. In other occasions, the problem is whether he should go to play to the park, because his father has told him that he should not go and Dad must be obeyed. So, very soon, the young boy or girl notices that there are two levels of things that ought to be done or avoided, as there are two levels of moral law: a fundamental one, because things should be that way, and a secondary one, because Dad says that going to play in the park may be dangerous.

This is to be a person. There must be a reason why humans act like that, and not like little dogs, crocodiles, or birds; why they are responsible and free; can love and hate; communicate in truth or in falsehood; act with a purpose in mind, and not out of compulsion; possess a sense of personal dignity; and find out that there is a law to be respected in their mutual relations; why they should be willing to accept obligations founded on authority considered to be legitimate. It is impossible to discern among animals not even one of the above-mentioned characteristics. Therefore, we have concluded ever since that there must be something that makes us specifically different from them.

We have already seen how Aristotle concluded that what gives man his specific difference with the rest of the animals is his rationality. There has never been anyone in his senses who, after seeing cave paintings made by our ancestors around 30,000 years ago, dares to suggest that they could have been painted by apes.

Because of our capacity to abstract intelligible notions from concrete sensible experiences, we are able to write papers like this one, speak of rights and wrongs, reflect on human nature, and build that monument of rationality that is a legal system.

2.3 Rational Sociability

It is obvious that persons are sociable; but so animals are. Relations among animals of the same kind are often based on mutual profit, on cooperation. Among different species that share the same grounds those relations are, most of the time, of sheer domination and destruction, according to the Darwinists and to the Marxists, although in many cases symbiosis or equilibrium prevails where individuals of different species need each other in order to survive.

But only humans decide, through reasonable choices, the kind of relationship with others that they want to enter into. At times they decide to cooperate, at times to destroy, at times to profit from each other; but in every instance there has been previous deliberation, a range of possibilities has been taken into account and free decisions have been made.

The social relations among persons ought to be established with rational and ethical considerations in mind. Social relations should not only be rational, since decisions to dominate, kill, plunder, or abuse are often rationally pondered; they must also be ethical, since they ought to respect the social order proper to persons. These relations must be such that they give to everyone what is due to him and everyone receives what is his right.

In primitive societies, custom sought to establish and to sanction what was proper behavior as it was commonly understood. But careful observation of the multiplication and complexity of the relations among town dwellers—civilization—led the Greek genius to conclude that, unless those mutual rights and duties were clearly stated and properly accepted and there was an effective way to enforce their fulfilment, the freedom and the dignity of the individual person was endangered, and the tranquility or order rendered impossible. The fruit of their reasonable philosophizing was the notion of **law**.

2.4 Law and Positive Law

Law is the ordination of reason for the common good, promulgated by those who legitimately take care of the community. *Quaedam rationis ordinatio ad bonum commune, ab eo qui curam communitatis habet, promulgata**[2]***. This classical definition of **positive law** has been a guiding light in the process of building Western civilization.

It encompasses a number of **features that must always be present in any real law: order**, right disposition among persons and among persons and things; it must be **rational**—follow right reason—which is another way of saying that respecting such order will bring about the intended effects; it **serves the common good**: *the sum to those conditions of social life which allow social groups and their individual members relatively thorough and ready access to their own fulfillment**[3]***; ought to be **promulgated**: formally published so that it can be sufficiently known to everyone affected; by the **legitimate authority**—those persons that every society has entitled to rule. The rationality of the positive law and its purpose, the common good, implies also that at the foundation of every piece of legislation there is a personal right that needs to be preserved, protected, enhanced, or developed.

We have already mentioned the existence of a double order of rights: some which belong to the person as such, ethical in nature, which are called **human rights**; others that result from man's insertion in a concrete society, and are **practical arrangements for the preservation, protection, enhancement, and development of those natural rights**, thought out by those whom the individual persons, by common agreement, have designated to perform that task.

An example will clarify the matter. A car is a convenient vehicle that allows us to go to other places faster and more comfortably than doing it afoot; but it is also a machine that can kill. Its disorderly use on the part of many brings about waste of time and resources. Other considerations aside, to drive a car could be close to a personal right, but needs to be regulated for everybody's good: for the safety of driver and the persons inside and outside it, who could be affected by the quality of the driving and in order to prevent others wasting time and money. Traffic laws, well thought out and implemented by legitimate authority, are adequate instruments to protect and guarantee the rights of the individual persons.

Although a double level of rights exists, it is accurate to talk of one level of positive law and a set of rights natural to persons; the adjective **natural** meaning that they are due to men for the sake of being men and nothing else: not dogs, rivers or crocodiles. But in using the term law in a partly the same and partly different sense—that is in an analogical way—we can affirm that the set of natural rights and duties, foundation of every other law, constitutes by itself a sort of transcendental law, ethical in nature, that a long tradition has designated as Natural Law.

The dualism of natural and positive rights connects respect for positive law with the virtue of justice; it makes a good man also a good citizen. It explains why a just law obliges and discredits any attempt to make human law autonomous by placing the legislative body or the Supreme Court in a place that belongs to God alone. Thomas More fulfilled his duties as a citizen by disobeying his King, in obedience to the law of his conscience.

2.5 Granted Rights

Natural rights cannot be granted by any human being, much less by any institution, since they are naturally possessed. To grant them is a show of infatuation with one's own power; to deny them constitutes an act of tyranny. Those who have granted others the right to live, or have attributed to themselves the power to deny the right to live are tyrants who have abused the power they enjoy: political assassinations, legislative acts that authorize abortion, lying for the sake of national prestige, genocide, depriving people of what belongs to them *in order to make a more profitable use of natural resources,* etc. are all abusive acts, ever more opprobrious when there is no human power to prevent them. No matter how they have been justified from the legal point of view they constitute acts of rational and voluntary regression to animal behavior, to the law of the strongest.

Legitimate authority has a limited power to grant legal rights and to impose legal duties to its subjects; it may do so as long as those rights and duties are specifications or practical applications of the natural rights; or at least when, with full respect for them, they contribute to enhance the good of the community and to the progress of civilization.

Respect for natural rights is not enough to make the granted rights or imposed duties to be in agreement with justice. It is also required that these rights and duties are properly distributed. The person constituted in authority is bond to give each one of his subjects what is due to him. Aquinas says that *distributive justice... distributes common good proportionally.* Difficult tasks! Because we are now speaking of an evaluated proportionality, the result not of computation, but of a prudential judgement that ought to take into account the particular conditions and circumstances of the subjects, the prudence of the person in authority and its values are paramount.

Not only it is necessary to be just in order to be good. A man constituted in authority will only practice distributive justice when he is truly good; when, besides a sense of fairness, he has self-control and possesses the necessary fortitude and wisdom, to the point that those who are in a position of governing others need to be good men in order to practice justice.

Legal rights often share of the imperfection that is proper to all human constructions. It is not possible for the law-giver to consider all personal situations; therefore, there can be instances where the human laws do not answer the plural considerations of space and time in which the subject finds itself. Thus, in such cases the fulfillment of the law morally cannot be exacted.

Once again what is naturally good, both personally and in relation with the common good, must prevail over granted rights and duties. A long Christian and Western tradition have supported the principle of the supremacy of **epikeia** over the letter of legal prescription, since it embodies the justice whose attainment is supposed to be the guiding intention of the human legislator. Epikeia is not a dispensation of the law, but a perfect realization of the legal justice; but only one who is a true lover of justice can discern how to use it without turning it into an excuse to fail in one's duty. It is the way a just and prudent legislator would have expressed the law if he would have been aware of that specific situation.

Notes

[1] Quoted by Pieper: The Four Cardinal Virtues. Page 43.
[2] Aquinas, Thomas. Summa Theologica, I-II Q.90, a. 4
[3] Vatican II. *Gauduim et Spes*, 26.1

3

Human Laws and Good Citizens

3.1 Citizens & Legitimate Authority

The term *city* entered the English language from the French *cité*, ultimately coming from the Latin *civitas.* Cicero wrote *concilia coetusque hominum iure sociali, quae civitates apellatur.* In other words, a city is an assembly of people brought together by law. Citizenship and law are two inseparable notions: when people assemble law there is a mob.

We must ask ourselves why people come together; why authority is needed; what makes it legitimate; and what is the purpose of promulgating laws.

To the question of **why people come together**, there are a variety of responses, although the only ultimately valid one, when they do it freely, is due to the fact that they are seeking a common good that, otherwise, is impossible or at least difficult to achieve.

There could be many other reasons for their assembling: they could be people interned in a concentration camp; or refugees escaping from the ravages of war; or it could simply be that they happened to find themselves in such a situation, for instance families living for centuries in a valley surrounded by high mountains. But these or other similar cases of coming or of being together are not necessarily intended; therefore, their assembling is purely passive.

Why do they need authority? For the Classics, *auctoritas* was the power of an auctor—an originator, a causer, an ancestor—to carry on his work; it was the *in-fluence* of the water source in the whole course of the river. Authority can be **natural**, as it is case of the parents with respect to their children; or it can be invested, **conferred** to a person by those who decide to group themselves for a common purpose. It is obvious that in so doing the citizens expect that individual to exercise authority within the **limits** that they have imposed on him and that he will make use of such authority exclusively for the **common good**. The granting of authority entails **no alienation** in the classical Fuerbach[1] manner, although it implies always a **risk of abuse**.

Authority is needed because the common good can only be achieved a certain unification of the wills of many, orienting them towards a common purpose. The exercise of authority aims to the unification of minds only to a certain extent, since the mind surrenders itself only to truth and in many debatable matters it is not easy, although it could be desirable, to reach a consensus.

Yet the exercise of authority is not exclusively founded on the *imperium*, **the right of ordering or commanding**, since the decisions have to correspond to ordinations of reason. In other words: a good, clearly recognizable and accepted aim can be attained in a variety of ways and the one in authority is empowered by the community to pass a prudential judgement about the most effective way to impose it on the others. To the exercise of legitimate authority, the subjects are committed to respond with another act of the will seeking union with it: this is an act of **obedience**, from the Latin *ob-oedire*, to listen, to pay attention to.

This aspect of rationality can never be absent from any human law: otherwise, it would lose its power to set a moral obligation of the individual in relation to the community.

What is it that makes authority to be legitimate? This question, presented in pure juridical terms, constitutes to a certain extend a kind of vicious circle, because the term **legitimate** means *according to law*. Therefore, anyone claiming to be endowed with authority must have acquired it according to preexisting laws; but is not clear why laws passed in previous generations may oblige us. That is why **real legitimacy** may always **include a moral aspect.**

The legitimacy of origin can, therefore, present a problem; history shows that it has been challenged on innumerable occasions. For some persons their authority derives from the fact of being the natural origin of their subjects, as in the case of parents in relation to their children. There could also exist a supernatural authority invested by God into a person as it was the case of Moses or Josuah.

Ordinarily it is the citizens the ones giving themselves the laws that regulate how a person is constituted in authority and how it is taken away from him; this is, in our understanding, the greatest merit of the democratic system. This system, though, rests on the assumption that the present-day citizens agree to the rules established by previous generations, which is something that cannot be taken for granted. Here we meet a problem that cannot be ignored.

In the historical monarchies, authority was oftentimes vested through lineage, not election, but the system was broadly accepted within certain conditions like swearing to honor the ancestral laws of the land, etc.

But the legitimacy of origin alone is not enough. **Legitimacy of exercise** is also needed: the exercise of authority must be confined within the bounds imposed by the community. For positive laws to impose ethical obligations upon the citizens this double legitimacy is a necessary, although not a sufficient, condition.

3.2 What Laws Should Intend to Achieve

What is what real, morally obliging laws should intend to achieve? In Western classical wisdom there is a broad consensus that only those legal impositions that are intended for the common good have the moral power to oblige. If the intention of the legal precept is not the common good, but only what is practical or pleasurable for the lawgiver or for a determined group (e.g., a social class, the population of a part territory, a political party, a bunch of friends, those who adhere to a certain ideology), then that specific piece of legislation is only formally a law, but lacks the intrinsic substance of a real law; in other words: it is an abuse of law; not a vehicle, but a miscarriage of justice, since it intends to infringe into the original freedom of the subjects for bastard reasons, the only legitimate reason for it being the common good.

Aristotle affirmed that *the intention of the lawgiver is to make good citizen***[2]**; the expression *good citizens* was meant to describe persons that can be considered good from the view point of their fulfillment of the established relations with other persons belonging to the same organized society.

Aquinas explains that a *law is nothing else but a dictate of reason in the ruler by whom his subjects are governed***[3]**. In other words, a man can be good only in so far as he follows the dictates of prudence, that tells him that something must be done or avoided, or that these or those means are fit to achieve a good end. Ordinarily the individual persons must pass their own judgements on these matters; but regarding those matters that refer to a common good that can only be obtained in cooperation, it would be practically impossible to achieve a consensus since there is plenty in them that is debatable. Therefore, the individual persons agree on transferring the responsibility of formulating the common rule of behavior to one or several persons chosen from among them, who are thus constituted in legislative authority.

Prudence being the right thinking about acting[4], it is clear that the laws, which are act of prudence of governance, must intend to lead the subjects to *their proper virtue,* that is to say to make them better men, by making them good in a particular aspect of their own activity.

To be a good citizen is therefore a part of being a good man; it would be impossible for a man to be good unless he tries to fulfill with exemplary perfection the legitimate laws of the land.

3.3 Human Laws Help Subjects to be Better Men

How do human laws work in helping the subjects to be better men? Aristotle says that *lawgivers make men good by contributing to the development of habits of doing good works*[5].

It is obvious that habits of external behavior can be imposed through coercion; but actions done under violence or fear are not true human actions, since for an action of a man to be truly human, it must be elicited from his intelligence and free will. The habits of doing good which the Philosopher speaks about are freely assumed habits: something appreciated and sought after, not something imposed by force.

How can human laws, therefore, contribute to make men better? They do so, first, by **enlightening the minds of the subjects**. Laws must possess a transparency of the good intended to achieve, or of the evil that is to be prevented. If the purpose of the law is not manifest or the adequacy between means and ends is not clearly presented, that piece of legislation fails to fulfill its primary purpose as law that is to enlighten the minds. When *the branches of the trees do not allow to see the forest,* such legislative puzzle can be a good occasion for legal practitioners to show their wits, but it defeats its own purpose as law.

What is good, when properly understood, always appeals to our nature; as a consequence, the common good that is intended by the law must be presented in such a way that it appeals to the wills of the subjects. And so human laws, when they are truly laws, help men to be better. Certainly, there must be in the laws an element of deterrence for those who are not willing to listen or to follow, as a way to protect the common good. Law, therefore, could be obeyed exclusively out of fear of punishment, but even in such cases there is some beginning of good in obeying them.

3.4 Bad Citizens

Those individuals who submit themselves to an authority in order to achieve an otherwise impossible common good are willing to practice a social virtue called **obedience to law**. The virtue of obedience, being a voluntary habit of doing good, implies no alienation, since it is personally assumed. The good citizen is happily obedient to true laws even when he is not totally in agreement with their formulation.

Even if the authority is legitimate in origin and exercise, disagreement of a citizen with the law can be founded on a number of reasons, mostly because he considers it unfit to bring forth the intended effects. He may consider that, even if its general objective is good, its particular aim is not well focused; or, what is even more frequent, that the means through which the lawgivers expects the law to achieve its aim are not perfectly adequate to its end. So, the good citizen is entitled to disagree with the existing law, to express his disagreement with due prudence and even to procure to change the law through legally established procedures, except in those cases when to manifest one's mind could cause great harm to the common good.

As long as there is only a defect of good, but no evil, the common good imposes on the good citizen an obligation to obey. The term **obligation** comes from the Latin *obligare*, to tie, to bind up. Originally *obligare* meant to bandage a wound: a very expressive way of indicating that the citizen feels voluntarily obliged to obey the laws in order to avoid social hemorrhage.

Here we touch the depth of human mystery: the human inclination to seek disorderly a partial good that breaks us away from contributing to the common good to the point of hurting it and, furthermore, from attaining one's ultimate personal good.

Human laws have ever since been characterized by possessing that power to coerce, to avoid that bad citizens may harm the common good. Here we can speak of a certain voluntary alienation, of a certain transfer of our intrinsic capacity to cause social evil to those in authority so that they may oblige us to avoid that harmful activity.

This remedy of what Christian thought has always considered to be a consequence of original and personal sins in us, makes use of the deterring power of fear to contain our inclination towards socially harmful behavior.

As for the justification of punishment itself, there has been and still there are a broad variety of opinions that go from atonement and just retribution all the way to the healing of the offender.

The bad citizen is not only bad because he does wrong things as a citizen; he has also entered voluntarily into a social agreement of accepting reasonable punishment if he breaks the rules that govern the common good—the **commonwealth** in English terms.

3.5 Bad Laws and Good Citizens

Men are always imperfect; therefore, they are perfectible and must try to be perfect. Human laws are perfectible, too. But human beings can also be bad and human laws can equally be bad. Not only they can, but some of them are actually bad in many countries otherwise endowed with a reasonably wholesome legal system.

Some laws can be bad, as we already saw, because they are unreasonable, unfit to serve their purpose: we have already mentioned them. Here it is enough to mention the fact that the proportion between reason and the lack of it can vary extraordinarily. Morally speaking, their force of obligation goes in proportion to their reasonableness, and can disappear completely when they are foolish. They could be designated as more or **less unreasonable laws**.

Never mind the severity of the punishment, that only indirectly serves as an indicator of the power to oblige possessed by the law. Moralists tend to dismiss the notion of **merely penal laws**[6], but I think that to deny the existence of a gradation of blinding force is to deny evidence: the same moralists jump over a red traffic light without scruples when there is no traffic, no danger to anyone, and the light appears to be out of order. What makes the law binding is not its having been approved and promulgated, but the fact of being *ordinatio rationis.*

Other laws can be bad because they have been promulgated by unlawful authorities or passed in an unlawful way; that is to say: they are **illegitimate**. And yet, they should not be discarded easily by the citizens, as long as they contribute to the common good: this could be the case, for example, of laws enacted by dictatorial regimes. A vacuum of law generates anarchy, which is a serious disease of the social body.

Finally, there are truly bad laws, because their aim is not the common good but some common evil that presents a good side as it usually happens with all human realities. If the evil is in the major premise, that is in the rejection of natural law, that law is in itself evil and **must be disobeyed**. This obligation to oppose an evil law is not excused by saying that one is obeying orders. Nazi concentration camps and St. Thomas More[7] are to examples that typify the bad and good citizen behavior.

Some other laws are bad because the means engineered by the law in order to achieve good purpose are bad in themselves. Forced sterilization could be an example of this kind. In these cases, the good objective, in so far as it is good, must be pursued; the means imposed by the law must be rejected, and alternative means should be sought after.

The good man must be a good citizen; he cannot have an ambiguous attitude in front of human law. He must love and respect it fully, while aware of its fallible nature; therefore, when obeying, rejecting, or interpreting the law he is passing a moral judgement that binds his conscience. The general moral law always prevails, providing its unique obligatory moral force upon the otherwise legitimate—but limited—power of coercion of human laws.

Notes

[1] Ludwig Feuerbach (1804-1872) claims that religion rises from one's alienation from oneself, and the projection of ideal qualities into a fictitious supreme "other".

[2] Aristotle. *Ethics*, II, 1.

[3] Aquinas. Summa Theologica, Q 92, reply.

[4] *Recta ratio agibilio.*

[5] Aristotle. Ethics, II, 1.

[6] This is the idea that some laws do not oblige in conscience: there is no ethical value attached to following them or not, although there is punishment attached to them if they are not fulfilled.

[7] Thomas More: "...in my conscience this was one of the cases in which I was bounden that I should not obey my prince, sinee that, whatsoever other folk thought of the matter (whose conscience and learning I would not condemn nor take upon me to judge), yet in my conscience the truth seemed on the other side."

4

Human Laws and the Power to Enforce Them

4.1 Power

Primarily, power means the capacity to do or accomplish something. Those constituted in authority in a human society must be endowed by the citizens with all the power that they need to be able to perform adequately the task entrusted to them. Such power, intrinsic to any authority, is primarily moral power, since the laws are addressed at the first instance to the conscience of the citizens, as set procedures through which the joint efforts of all can bring good results for the whole community. The legislators study every matter according to prudence and decide about a course of action, which good citizens are willing to accept as their own decision.

Since there are always some citizens not ready to do so, authority could become ineffective if it is not invested with the physical—or psychological—power to enforce the law. To place someone in a position of authority always entails placing in his hands a certain amount of physical power that he can make use of, without any further limitations that those imposed by the existing laws. It is a power to coerce, to compel by force or intimidation, without regard for the individual desire or volition.

Without power, authority will be frequently disobeyed unless the subjects are men of great moral standards and, when order is broken, society will fall into disarray, since to reestablish order may not be easy. Those who govern should have at their disposal as much power as it is needed in order to fulfill effectively the task entrusted to them.

4.2 The Moral Dimension of the Use of Power

By itself, from a moral perspective, power is neither good nor bad; but its handling can be good or bad according to the purpose for which it is used and the way it is used.

In the present existential condition of man—the one that Christian thought describes ad fallen nature—there is almost in every human being a tendency to accumulate power in order to satisfy one's ego by imposing on others one's will, deriving from it advantages of self-gratification. Those in authority are easily inclined to seek privilege, to place themselves outside the limits of the law. Ultimately that capacity to impose one's will that accompanies authority can easily lead those constituted in authority to ignore those characteristics of rationality and destination to the common good that justify its existence and exercise.

The possibilities of abuse of legal power can be very many, not to mention the possibilities of abuse of power in general. It is said that when Alexander the Great was dying at the age of 33, after having conquered half of the known world, he was asked who among his generals should be his successor. He answered: "Let the strongest command." The result was the immediate destruction of the political edifice he had painstakingly built.

Compare this story with another one attributed to St. Thomas Aquinas. The chapter of the Dominicans was meeting to elect a new Master General. He was asked his opinion about three candidates:

one known for his holiness, another one known for his learning, and the third one known to be a very prudent man. Aquinas answered: "Let the holy man sanctify us; let the learned man teach us; but the one who govern us should be a prudent man." Which shows that, in his opinion, political prudence is the characteristic virtue of the man of government.

This is true for the executive power, that must apply the law to particular circumstances; but, with more reason, it applies to legislators, whose mission is to envision a rational ordination, an *ordinatio rationis.*

Of its own nature, power is blind; only reason can give a sense of purpose to its use. Therefore, to harness power, keep it under control, use it with moderation, and establish the necessary mechanism to avoid its possible abuse constitutes a primordial moral obligation: a mechanism that must possess its own authority and its own independent source of power.

4.3 Power to Enforce the Laws

Similar considerations, passing through Montesquieu, have become the foundation of the standard praxis of the democratic countries. In Christian Europe, up to the appearance of totalitarian tendencies during the Enlightenment period of the XVIII Century, the executive powers, except in what referred to warfare, were spread along the social body: there was no concentration of power in the executive. The Monarch was Supreme Judge, and the Legislative power resided in occasional Parliaments, *Cortes*, and the like.

The Customs of the peoples prevailed as source of law. According to St. Augustine[1] "the customs of God's people and the institutions of our ancestors are to be considered as laws." *The actions of the people—Aquinas comments—especially when they are repeated so as to make a custom, obtain the force of law.* And he finishes saying that *accordingly, custom has the force of law, abolishes law, and is the interpreter of law.*

That is why, when the social order was replaced by the modern order of nations that abolish privilege (i.e., private law) and concentrated the executive power in the State, it became imperative to impose a strict division of powers, whose main purpose was to let the people establish their own laws and let the exercise of the executive power be controlled by the laws. The coercive power needed to enforce the law was also independently administered.

The solution was mostly correct, yet it could not avoid conflictive situations, because what decides the content of the laws is, at the end, the will of the majority of legislative representatives. The majority's will, not the intellectual consensus; quite often the majority represents an ideological group and, consequently, the common will is not even the majority's will but simply the party line. The law, instead of being an *ordinatio rationis,* becomes a decision of the will, an act of political power; this does not mean that the intelligence of the representatives has not been operational but that, not infrequently, it has been directed not towards the common good but towards the achievement of an ideological objective.

4.4 Ideologies and the Common Good

One can expect an irritated reaction on the part of someone, at hearing that the democratic system of government runs the risk of substituting ideologies for the natural law as the ultimate source of legislation. Remember what we saw at the beginning of these lectures that every human law is a practical application of a precept of the natural law to specific circumstances. I imagine hearing something like "the ideologies, too, aim at the common good."

Let us start from the beginning: **What are ideologies?** The standard definition is that they are a body of doctrine, myth, belief, etc. that guides an individual, social movement, institution, class, or large group. As a well-defined concept, modern ideologies appeared when the consensus of Christian principles disappeared in the Western world. Liberalism, Capitalism, Nationalism, Fascism, Marxism, Socialism, Communism, took the place of the old social order as a pattern and system of ideas to guide the organization of the world.

They aimed at filling the vacuum left by the rejection of the *ius populorum Christianum* founded in the existence and the acceptance of a common human nature, or rather they tried to configure a new man for a new social order. They claimed that the idea of man upon which Christendom had been built did not correspond to the reality of man.

To start with, they rejected the notion of human nature, since it was impossible—according to them—to know what man is; but they established instead postulates that described men as mere consumers, pleasure seekers, cells of larger social bodies, contented animals, or other paradigms. Therefore, social structures should be conformed to meet their description of the ideal of man: there was no definition since there was nothing essential to men.

Some went even further and concluded that there was no notion that possessed a definite value, and therefore, the beauty of a democratic society was in the absence of principle, the frivolous and enjoyable game of inventing always new structures and exploring new forms. The only principle that had to be respected was the form, not the substance, the acceptance of the rules of the game, although there were some that, considering that those rules were good in themselves, did not reject the possibility that others could build up different societies under different rules of the game.

4.5 Conflicts and Ideologies

The principle that governed ideologies had to produce necessarily conflicting contradictions among them. It was natural that things should be this way, although the term **natural** had to be carefully avoided. They solved this problem by developing philosophical systems that denied the principle of non-contradiction and permitted something to be at the same time true and false.

They were systems based on half-crazy truths, characterized by radical positions: denied the evidence, took the part for the whole, and rejected any dialogue with common sense or with accepted wisdom.

To conclude that ideologies where without effectiveness would be mistaken: in fact, the opposite is true. They were as effective as an explosion for levering a hill. All energies concentrated in a direction, they achieved wonders of good and evil at the same time: National Socialism brought back its power and sense of national pride to the German nation, getting her out of the humiliation and pessimism caused by the Treaty of Versailles, at the price of the Holocaust; Napoleonic Liberalism swept off many obsolete social structures, but decimated the Spanish and Russian population; Mao's version of Marxism unified China, at the expense of, perhaps, twenty million victims; Communism modernized Russia, but created the Gulags; the Capitalism of the Industrial Revolution built up powerful industries, while bringing misery to traditional artisans and originated the so-called social problem; Liberal Democratic ideology fostered effectively the defense of human rights, but simultaneously introduced abortion laws that every year terminate the lives of a multitude of innocent citizens-to-be, in the most prosperous nations of the world.

The list is endless and should lead us to reflect why ideologies have been at the same time the cause of real progress and of man-made catastrophes. Some ideologists claim that such is the unavoidable consequence of the dialectics of thesis, antithesis, and synthesis—just the way things work—while for those who deny man's spiritual nature, those excesses are the logical outcome of the survival of the fittest.

The current ideologists tend to be indulgent with those of the past who happen to be at the same side of the swinging of the pendulum and blame the crimes and horrors on practical mistakes or errors of perception. Would not it be more logical to conclude that every attempt to reduce man to only one of the aspects of his complex but unified being, looking at him exclusively as *homo animalis, politicus, oeconomicus,* a pleasure seeker, a wolf to another man, a noble savage, a victim of social regulations, a portion of matter in its dialectical way towards perfect equality, etc. brings necessarily chaos in the long term?

The ideologies came to fill up a vacuum left by a vision of man built through the joint effort of Revelation and human rationality, which was purposely blurred by men who thought it a more worthy project that man should try to take over God's place.

Now-a-days not a few intellectuals claim that the end of the era of the ideologies is at hand: mankind has taken a painful beating for having yielded to those phantasms that sick minds have induced many to accept as alternative models of the **modern man**. Rationalism tried to usurp the place of right reason, but its radical falsehood was shown in its corrupted fruits.

Unfortunately, there are clear signs that the weak, self-proclaimed, non-ideological attitudes predominant today constitute another *de facto* covert ideology: a new attempt to reduce man to a mere pleasure seeker absolutely unsure of anything beyond his selfish drives.

4.6 Legislation as an Instrument of Power Used to Configure Man and Society

Whenever the ideology of a party usurps the place that belongs to natural law, oftentimes it supplies the major premise of the new pieces of legislation. The ideology that gives coherence to the party that controls the legislative body, demands complete subservience of its members: under the excuse of the need of party unity or of maintaining the majority in the legislative body, power becomes more important than justice and truth; at least from time-to-time things occur this way. Laws that are promulgated under such kind of pressure are neither rational ordinations nor true manifestations of the will of the majority, but only the result of bending to the tyrannical will of a small clique ideologists.

The history of the 19th and 20th Centuries in many nations of the civilized world could easily be written under this perspective. Even if specific ideologies not always managed to prevail in informing totally the contents of legislation as long as the democratic guaranties were in place, there were a few occasions when those who reached power through democratic channels passed new laws that were in fact intended as means of political oppression either by abolishing the democratic safeguards of the system or by ensuring an effective social control through mob pressure, police, propaganda, education, and the media, and by means of constant threats to the safety and welfare of those institutions that could oppose the totalitarian ambitions of the group in power.

In most cases, though, the normal thing was a constant tug-of-war between the different conflicting ideologies and the classical idea of man's nature. When in power, the adherents to different ideologies tried to reshape the world according to their own idea of man. Constant changes in the systems of ownership, undisguised attempts to monopolize education and social welfare, imposition of suffocating conditions to the activities of the religious bodies, *nationalization* of institutional property, abolition of old-established legitimate municipal, regional, or professional privileges, cultural and educational *guidance* exerted from the centers of power, campaigns in favor of birth control and abortion, self-attribution of power on the part of the legislators over the institution of the family, financial sanctions imposed on the dissenters, and a long etc. that one day will be seen with horror as the ugly side of the so-called modern man.

The noble task of legislating, whose original purpose was to defend the freedom of the individual persons and natural social groups, has been transformed into a tool of social engineering. Certainly, the fast pace of contemporary history, required many legal innovations but in no few occasions this urgency degenerated into legislative diarrhea: civil society could hardly assimilate the meaning and value of so many pieces of legislation, to the point that law, as such, rather than helping ordinary men to be good citizens, became an esoteric tool in the hands of law specialists, trying to outwit each other and to collect fat fees.

What should have been a service to freedom and to justice ended up as a tool of dominance. Natural law imposes no other limitations than those proper to our own human sociable being, but ideologies turn men into slaves or into animals competing for self-satisfaction. What is worse, they try to impose a different perception of reality, a real brain washing, with the help of the media, control of education, and the conforming power of the laws.

In the pendular swing of ideologies, human nature always marks the center and ends winning the day—but not without leaving the ground covered with cadavers.

Notes

[1] Aquinas. Summa Theologica, I-II, q. 47, art. 3

5

Legal Positivism: Introduction

5.1 An Epistemological[1] Problem

As we saw, natural law imposes on us men moral obligations, but most of those patronizing ideologies do it under the premise that human nature, even if it existed, would be unrecognizable by the human mind.

They base their assumption in an old epistemological quarrel that started with the Nominalism of William of Ockham[2] , a Briton rebel friar who considered that concepts were mere names without any real content; but he was a mediaeval man, the end of the old world.

Descartes[3], instead, was the beginning of a new thinking in which men gradually took the place of God[4] .The first serious steps in this direction was to deny the capacity of the human intellect to reach the essence of things and was taken by the British Empiricists: according to them, we only perceive sensations and are unable to go further than that. Therefore, we can feel how things act but not know what they are.

Nevertheless, the good luck of Isaac Newton[5] led him to prove that there were physical laws that are always fulfilled and his findings undermined the empiricist proposal. An answer was propounded by Emmanuel Kant[6]: the foundation of the universal and necessary knowledge—as opposed to the particular and contingent—does not proceed from the reality of things, but from the inside of the human mind. Other thinkers radicalized his thought excluding the reality of the things themselves: reality was only a creation of the human mind, and so man was creator.

As for the moral obligations, Kant thought that the practical reason is autonomous; that morality is based not on reality, but on the structure of the mind itself.

The post-kantian Idealist went further and made the human mind not only the source of morality, but the creator of all things. The Marxists, went even further to make the revolutionary praxis not only the creator of all things, but also the criterion of truth.

Most of the modern non-Christian thought has lost contact with reality. It rests on the **principle**—rather a postulate—of **immanence**, that states that man is only conscious of his own awareness and there is no way to jump from it to reality. To speak of human nature and morality founded on the being of things, and ultimately on God, is for them nonsense.

5.2 Copying from a Great Little Book

I am referring to Charles Rice's **50 Questions on the Natural Law**[7]. There it is plainly expressed how modern Legal Positivism came to be.

"Allan Bloom, in his introduction to *The Closing of the American Mind,* observed that, for American university students the relativism of truth is not a theoretical insight, but a moral postulate, the condition for a free society." Which means that, unless we do not believe in anything, we cannot live in peace with one another.

Relativism of truth means that truth, instead of being adequacy between mind and reality, as classical Western thought teaches, is a purely subjective vision of always elusive phenomena; it postulates that, since we human beings cannot be sure of anything, the most that we can have is educated opinions about which a compromise is always possible.

It is surprising that those sponsoring such a view—which according to Bloom are most of Amerian university students—have not arrived at it at the end of a long epistemological research, but have input it in their outlook in life as a ***moral postulate***: which means, in other words, that since they want to create a better world, where everyone can think and do whatever he wants—that is what is perceived a **free society** to be—their decision of never taking anything as true is something that the members of the social body must blindly accept in order to be good citizens. The place of the truth and good is taken by what is **politically correct**.

Yet it only seems to mean that. Under a closer scrutiny, it is obvious that the meaning of **free society** is not for them what it seems to be at face value. First, because the absence of truth must be **imposed** as a moral starting point; and second, because those who postulate it do not renounce to pass laws, many laws, destined to change the world; laws that will be mercilessly obligatory as long as they are passed according to democratic rules carefully avoiding any reference to truth: the necessary and sufficient reference is social majority.

All this could be summarized by saying that their proposal consists in abolishing truth so that the majority can impose their will on the minority. Naturally, the democratic system guarantees that this will happen only for a while, since one of the fundamental rules of the game is that the opinions that conform majorities and minorities are in a constant state of flux.

5.3 A Comparative Evaluation

The classical foundation of law was based on the conviction of the existence of some fundamental moral truths on which the majority of good men agree, and that our certainties about them had been strengthened by divine Revelation. Those truths were simple: man is free to seek God according to the dictates of his own conscience; parents are primarily responsible for their children; subjects must honor and obey their legitimate superiors; life and body's integrity must be respected, likewise other people's property; solemn statements must be truthful and commitments must be honored; the family must be protected; there must be solidarity in society; and the right of self-determination of individuals and minor groups should not be trespassed unless the common good really demands it. All this was called natural law.

When men obeyed these laws, they behaved like real good men in their mutual relations. Now, the peoples of the world selected those they thought were their best men so that, ingeniously, they would devise ways and means to apply these laws to the specific circumstances of their times and places. But American university students-not all of them, we hope-think that it is imperative to eliminate such reference to a universally accepted principle-fruit of experience and guaranteed by divine Revelation because in this way men will be beyond good and evil, will be law unto themselves. In other words, revolting against the law of God, they make themselves free. That brings to us a reminder of the Biblical temptation: You will be like God, beyond good and evil.[8]

Once the notion of natural law had been rejected as a foundation of the positive laws, there were still a number of attempts to find some alternative foundation to them. Some thought that it could be man's natural inclination to gratify himself and his no less natural tendency to supremacy. Pressure of the environment and survival of the fittest were supposed to be the foundations of all human behavior, while the rule of law was limited to guarantee that people did not interfere excessively with one another in their search for satisfaction and in the struggle for natural selection. What was being proposed was a sort of restricted application of the laws that regulate animal relations.

The difficulty was to determine what were the reasons for and what should the extent of such restriction. If happiness would take the place of pleasure there seemed to be nothing to object to the first portion of the formulation except, perhaps, that any happiness beyond physical pleasure had to be spiritual in nature which implied a recognition that human nature included a spiritual component. What will happen when the physical pleasure sought after by a man conflicted with the virtue sought after by another?

To accept that survival of the fittest could stand as a human absolute had more serious consequences. The *homo homini lupus**[9]*—man is a wolf to man—stated by Hobbes[10], an English Empiricist himself, easily led to the conclusion that man, left to himself, will act as a predator to other human beings, which is the reverse of true civilization. In other words, as the Spanish saying goes, *el pez grande se come al chico*—big fish eat little fish[11]. It just happened that the sponsors of this kind of philosophy, otherwise known as Liberals, were mostly on the side of the "big fish" and, as a consequence, the small fish decided that Liberalism was inimical to them and they must do something about it. Yet we cannot but to be grateful to the Liberal ideology for having rediscovered forcefully the transcendental importance of human freedom that the classical notion of human nature included as one of its most characteristic features, but that somehow had been lost with it.

*Little fish of the world, unite!**[12]*, was the rallying cry of the little fish, when the lack of restrain of the big ones threatened their kind.

For the sponsors of this new philosophy, the only important thing was to preserve and to foster the species. To develop well-fed, contented animals, all equal to each other, was the radical law for such endeavor. The only purpose of law was to prevent the danger that no specimen will end up being superior in any way to others and try to dominate them, thus disturbing the harmony of the herd.

The law must be inflexible and demanded no restriction. The only *slight problem* was to determine who was to apply the law. He who applies the law ought to possess a power that the other men could not possess, defeating in this way the law of equality. In fact, those who possess such power could be in a position to *engulf and devour* even more easily than the big fish of the opposite system did to the small ones, since their power was supposed to be absolute. Unfortunately, they did *engulf and devour* ***[13]*** and no one could contest their actions and no element of rationality was going to remain beyond the will of the group constituted as Messiahs of the new Socialist order whose main objective was to remain in power.

That **human solidarity** is an important value is beyond question: in fact it is the main purpose for human society. Once again, the point was the extent and the manner of exercising authority and what would be the basis for that traditional behavior that is the key to understanding how society must be constituted. Neither the wild beasts' laws nor the ants' laws seemed to provide the answer, for the sole reason that men are neither wild beasts nor ants.

5.4 A Surprising Twist: A Proposal for Abolishing Truth as the Foundation of Society

We go back to Allan Bloom's description of contemporary cultural attitudes among American university students: "Relativism is necessary to openness; and this is the virtue, the only virtue, which all primary education for more than fifty years has dedicated itself to inculcating. Openness—and the relativism that makes it the only plausible stance in the face of various claims to truth and various ways of life and kinds of human beings—is the great insight of our times. The true believer is the real danger. The study of history and of culture teaches that all the world was mad in the past; men always thought they were right, and that led to wars, persecutions, slavery, xenophobia, racism, chauvinism. The point is not to correct the mistakes and really be right; rather it is not to think you are right at all. The students, of course, cannot defend their opinion. It is something with which they have been indoctrinated. The best they can do is to point out all the opinions and cultures there are and have been. What right, they ask, do I or anyone else have to say one is better than the others?"

The radical opposition of the two great contemporary ideologies brought wars and millions of deaths. As it happened when the religion wars devastated Europe in the XVII Century, today's men have leaned towards skepticism: this is not a new phenomenon.

What is new is the proposal of making of relativism—which is another term for absence of all certainty—the fundamental, rather the **only virtue** of our times. Observe carefully that it is not said to be the only truth, which would be a contradiction in terms, and the new Skeptics are in no way fond of Dialectics.

Why should relativism be the only virtue is an important question that requires an answer, in spite of the manifest anti-rationalism of its proponents. Should the term virtue mean something, it can only be that cultivating skepticism is the right way of acting because men, in order to survive and to be happy, must live at peace with each other and should therefore carefully avoid what may disturb that peace.

But for skepticism to be the ruler of behavior, something has to be imposed upon all men and there are only two ways of doing so. One, by indoctrination, a lengthy process of bringing forth a new type of thinking man, freely willing not to be sure of anything, an old utopia of impossible results, since men have the persistent tendency of getting to the bottom of things: up to now, all ideologies have tried to create a new man but to no avail.

In the meantime, the other method has to be employed: those who are convinced that the only solution to men's problems is to remove from them the pernicious habit of looking for the ultimate explanation of things, have to make use of all available means of institutional and psychological pressure to oblige them to follow a social system that may, in due time, lead to perfect relativism: such system is **democracy without moral content** founded on legal positivism, whose preservation justifies the use of power: To respect the rules of the democratic game becomes then the only moral rule; and the use of power is justified against those who threaten them. As it always happens, that way of thinking is not without merits. Tolerance in matters open to free opinion, which are many, is an absolute need for men to live at peace with one another; and peace—the tranquility of order—is at the apex of the common good.

Yet, tolerance alone does not seem to guarantee peace among men, since peace is only possible when there is justice: *Opus justitiae, pax,* said the classics. Men cannot suffer indefinite abuse and injustice until that day when all men of the world decide to become tolerant and respectful to each other. Therefore, it seems that at least for the time being the laws of the nations must protect that justice is lived in the relations among men, and power must be used to make sure that those laws are respected, and that those who try to take advantage of the benign and tolerant dispositions of good citizens, get the opportune correction and punishment if needed.

We conclude this review going back to the origin of our reflections, to the point where Classical thought left us: that for men to live at peace, society as such must guarantee a climate of mutual tolerance and justice and that, in order to protect that justice without which peace is rendered impossible, the legislators need to take into account what is due to them: relativism is a recipe for tyrannical and arbitrary use of power, since only the faithful consideration of what by nature is due to man can allow his true freedom to blossom.

Therefore, there should be in society as much freedom as it is possible and compatible with the common good. Of course, the rules of the democratic game seem to be better fit than any other possible rules to protect the right exercise of power: the extent of education, information, and communications make democratic government now-adays almost inevitable. Therefore, political power must see to it that the rules of the democratic game are respected although always conscious that they are somehow conventional rules submitted to the historical circumstances and not moral values.

5.5 The Gradual Melting Down of a System without Fulchrum

Societies do not collapse at once—not at least in most cases: they melt down little by little. The reason is that no matter how the ideologists push relativism, the individual men are guided by their consciences more than by propaganda. Not many months ago, the *International Herald Tribune* carried an article of one of its customary columnists[14]. That man, a little more than middle-aged, seasoned in activities of anti-Communist propaganda and a typical representative of generation of the Berkeley and Nanterre revolutions of the 60's, wondered what could be the reason why more than a million young people met in Paris to listen to an aging Pope in the World Youth Day. He wondered if all of them went to Mass on Sundays. Why did they come?—he asked himself. He concluded that they came because the generation of their parents—himself one of them—had promised them happiness in sex without limits, absence of rules, riches and self-gratification; but they had the experience of broken families, abortions, the pains and inner decay brought about by drug abuse, the emptiness of nothing to look for. So, they were listening to that old man because he seemed to be the only one with certainties, and were happy when he imposed on them demands of an upright and fruitful life.

Notes

[1] *Episteme* is the Greek for *knowledge.* Epistemology is the study of the nature and origin of knowledge: How human beings can have a true mental grasp of reality outside themselves.

[2] 1300?-49

[3] 1596-1650

[4] Descartes intended to build a philosophical system based on principles which are certain, followed by logical deductions, Mathematics-like; for the he applies a method is systematic doubt of anything which is not "clear and distinct." His starting point is the famous *cogito ergo sum*: I think, therefore, I am. By placing the starting point of Philosophy in thought, he triggered off a philosophical approach as IMMANENTISM (i.e., to remain within), which has dominated the intellectual panorama of the world for the past 350 years: a true intellectual dead-end.

[5] 1642-1727

[6] 1724-1804

[7] Ignatius Press, 1996

[8] Gen 3, 6

[9] Plautus, a Roman dramatist (c. 250-184 BC), is the first in living memory to have put this thought in writing: *Lupus est homo homini, non homo, quom qualis sit non novit.* A man is a wolf rather than a man to another man, when he has not yet found out what he is like. Interestingly enough this classical quotation, repeated many times later on as *Homo homini lupus,* implies that only by knowing what man is—i.e., his nature—can his behavior be truly worthy of himself, truly human.

[10] Political Philosopher (1588-1679)

[11] Also a well-known English proverb.

[12] The proletarians have nothing to lose but their chains. They have a world to win. ***Working men of all countries unite!*** Closing words of The Communist Manifesto (1848) by Karl Marx (1818-83) and Friedrich Engels (1820-95)

[13] The sheep, that were so meek and tame, and so small eaters now, become so great devourers, and so wild, that they eat up and swallow the very men themselves. To use, in prophetic mode, the words of Thomas More in Utopia.

[14] William Pfaff

6

Legal Positivism

6.1 In Search for a Justification of a Behavior

We have seen how the political, moral, and educational mood of a huge portion of contemporary Western culture is to cultivate—and even to impose—tolerance as the basis of social peace, a kind of tolerance that requires the abolition of truth as a moral postulate.

Now a postulate is, by definition, a proposition whose truth is admitted without proof, that is needed as a foundation for further reasoning. To propose the abolition of truth would have been a contradiction in terms, that is why the adjective *moral* had to be added to the noun *postulate*, giving to it a completely new meaning: the one of a decision of the will without any rational content. It was not a truth needed to serve as the root of a well-proven tree of truths, but a command of the will that was thought necessary to bring peace to mankind.

No one has ever proven that tolerance alone has ever brought peace to any human society, not at least in our historical records. We have already seen that an elementary analysis of men's behavior demonstrates that the achievement of peace requires not only tolerance but above all justice, a moral reality filled with a definitive and strong rational content.

That is why the claims of absolute tolerance and abolition of truth as a need for peace seemed to have arisen above all among young libertines sponsored and encouraged by equally libertines intellectuals. Their position did not sprout as much from theory as from praxis. Their rallying cry—make love not war—points out clearly in that direction. Theirs was a weak thought, a feeling rather, an excuse for sex and drugs, mixed with a genuine desire for peace and concern for the ecology. Liberals who had run out of bounds, they brought forward the ultimate conclusions of Rousseau's utopia.

Now, this mood of the times needed a justification because the big majority of the people of the civilized world still enjoyed sufficient dosages of sanity to perceive that feeling alone was a recipe for disaster. The justification had been provided by Hans Kelsen[1] and it was through him that those basically anti-juridical ideas have shrewdly penetrated into the legal system.

6.2 An Epistemological Alibi

Kelsen had gone through the catastrophe of World War II, justified by the aggressors in the name of ideology, something that he equaled to strong certainties, and therefore he sponsored as a remedy for further follies a concept of law founded on a gentle skepticism. He called it "philosophical relativism which advocates the empirical doctrine that reality exists only within human knowledge, and that, as the object of knowledge, the thing itself is beyond human experience; it is inaccessible to human knowledge and therefore unknowable"[2] He rejected philosophical absolutism, the metaphysical view that there is an absolute reality, i.e., a reality that exists independently from human knowledge.

There was little novelty in Kelsen's *philosophical relativism.* His immanentism was already implicit in the English Empiricists and had already matured in Kant's mind two hundred years before. After him, most of the thinkers of the Western world who did not adhere to the Classical tradition, were immanentists in one way or another; there was even an attempt of a few Christian thinkers, known as Modernists, to put together Faith and immanentism although their teaching was soon rejected by the Magisterium, as incompatible with revealed truth. America, dominated by second-rate philosophical schools—Dewey, W. James—had never taken very seriously those European vagaries; it was more inclined to a pragmatic way of thinking.

On the other hand, after more than a century of abhorring Metaphysics, the notion of being reappeared in Europe by the hand of Heidegger[3] and—horror!—this distinguished professor had been a collaborator of the Nazis. And so, the combined result of the anti-metaphysical fad and the empirical-pragmatic Anglo-Saxon tradition, made Kelsen thought palatable in the political and juridical circles of the nation and soon was going to lead the Western World.

Kelsen convinced the Americans that epistemological realism was identical to political absolutism and that democracy required the abolition of objective truth; as a result, the political and juridical establishments opted to accept that truth was unattainable and that the only guarantee of world peace was the forceful defense of the rules of the democratic game that implied a total rejection of any claim to possess moral truth. Let us listen to Kelsen.

6.3 Reading Kelsen

"For just as autocracy is political absolutism and political absolutism is paralleled by philosophical absolutism, democracy is political relativism which has its counterpart in philosophical relativism."[4]

"If one believes in the existence of the absolute, and consequently in absolute values, in the absolute good (...) is it not meaningless to let a majority vote decide what is politically good? (...) Tolerance, minority rights, freedom of speech and freedom of thought, so characteristic of democracy, have no place within a political system based on the belief in absolute values. This belief irresistibly leads—and it has always led—to a situation in which the one who assumes to possess the secret of the absolute good claims to have the right to impose his opinion as well as his will upon others who are in error. And to be in error is, according to this view, to be wrong and hence punishable." We do not need to extrapolate too far to conclude that, for Kelsen, God himself was a nuisance for human coexistence and his commandments tyranny. Now comes the unavoidable.

"If, however, it is recognized that only relative values are accessible to human knowledge and human will, then it is justifiable to enforce a social order against reluctant individuals only if this order is in harmony with the greatest possible number of equal individuals, that is to say the will of the majority."

The two portions of this last affirmation are really puzzling. First, Kelsen concludes that the application of force in order to impose a certain social behavior depends on a conditional—even if false—proposition. "If only relative values are accessible to man... "According to Webster's Dictionary, the ethical meaning of the term **value** is "any object or quality **desirable** as a means or as an end in itself," the idea of value implying therefore, an element of subjectivity, of personal appreciation, of something necessarily relative. But it does not exclude the possibility that the object or quality appreciated possesses something in itself that makes it to be appreciable, especially when it makes reference to persons. Even if someone does not like greatly people from a certain race or nationality, this does not entitle him to maltreat them, because the fact is that those people are objectively valuable regardless of his personal judgement. And second, the expression "then it is justifiable to enforce a social order against reluctant individuals only if this order is in harmony with the greatest possible number of equal individuals" is simply a monstrosity. The majority of people of Sodom and Gomorrah wanted Lot to deliver his visitors to them so that they could satisfy their homosexual appetites. What about if the majority of the Germans wanted to exterminated the Jews?

Listen to Kelsen; "The legal order of totalitarian states authorizes their governments to confine in concentration camps persons whose opinions, religion or race they do not like; to force them perform any kind of labor, even to kill them. Such measure may be morally or violently condemned; but they cannot be considered as taking place outside the legal order of those states."[5] As a consequence, "From the point of view of the science of law, the law under Nazi government was law. We may regret it but we cannot deny it was law."[6]

Brutal as it may look, this conclusion only implies a change **in the notion of law that, according to Kelsen, should be thought as an ordination, either rational or otherwise, as long as it is consistent, imposed by those democratically placed in charge of the community, regardless of the purpose of such imposition**. The notion of law, emptied of real content, gets reduced to pure formalism and includes those legal dispositions that have always been considered as **democratic tyranny.**

We look in vain for an explanation of Kelsen's statement that the majority is empowered to impose its will on the minority without limits, except that they are more: probably he does not offer any. Since, according to him, no one can be sure of anything, all can be reduced to a matter of power of enforcement. It would have been more logical, perhaps, to say that law is an ordination, either rational or not, imposed by those who possess in the community the power to enforce it, regardless of the purpose of such imposition. This is the logical result of eliminating from the idea of law the ethical considerations of rationality of ordination and of destination to the common good and this is what all tyrants in history have done.

6.4 Biased Kelsen

There is more in this Professor of Vienna, Cologne, Prague, Harvard, and Berkeley that plain attachment to a purely formal science of law, emptied from practical considerations. His driving force seems to have been horror to any form of absolutism. A system based on the belief in absolute values "irresistibly leads—and has always led—to a situation in which the one who assumes to possess the secret of the absolute good claims to have the right to impose his opinion as well as his will upon the others who are in error."[7] Horror to absolutism is something that all of us cannot but share thoroughly with him, but the rest of his reasoning has serious flops.

What about if a part of this certainty of the existence of an absolute good and of our ability to know it no matter how imperfectly, includes the conviction that our Creator has left most of the social issues open to the free discussion of men, and therefore, a big portion of this absolute consists precisely in upholding men's freedom to negotiate among ourselves the rules governing our social life in common? Certainly, this freedom cannot be unlimited, since each of us is limited by ourselves and has limits imposed on him by others; This is the reason why we are social beings and our sociability must be regulated by laws. Remember Archimedes: *Give me a fulcrum and I will move the earth.* The existence of some certainties not only does not impair freedom, but rather renders it possible.

Paradoxically, Kelsen cannot avoid at least a couple of certainties: that we cannot be sure of anything is one of them; and the other is that the majority has the right to impose its will on the minority without any other reference to rationality or to the common good. This second one is more difficult to accept.

Certainly, one must agree with him that the democratic system has, in general, advantages over other historical systems, because on it "the minority must have a chance to express freely their opinion and must have full opportunity of becoming the majority."

But he continues: "Only if it is not possible to decide in an absolute way what is right and what is wrong it is advisable to discuss the issue and, after discussion, to submit to a compromise."[8] The logical conclusion of this premise is not that a compromise will be reached but rather that, no matter how wrong the will of the majority, it will always be imposed on the minority, after having politely listened to its arguments; at least this is what happens in practice. Democracy without an ethical foundation not only does not avoid tyranny, but rather unavoidably ends up producing it, although it always provides a chance that the moral arguments of the minority may at the end be accepted by a majority as long as they still believe that there are forms of behavior that are right and others that are wrong. But, if the reasoning is about what is right and what is wrong, ultimately the aim of the law-maker is to structure society according to those ethical **principles**, or at least opinions, of the larger group.

Now, absence of principle should logically imply the abolition of the Constitution of the Supreme Court. First because it embodies some fundamental **principles** which cannot be easily submitted to discussion, and second because the most important issues are left in the hands of the prudential judgement of a few. But to abolish these institutions will mean the melting down of the whole system, bringing us back to the very beginning of the problem that we have been considering and which is double-faced. Its negative side is a sort of Gödel's theorem[9] applied to juridical systems: none of them can be self substaining; while the positive side is that, even if the consideration of the natural law as fulcrum of a system does not guarantee that such system is bullet-proof to error, misunderstanding, and abuse, when combined with democracy it permits a dialogue between majority and minority in which both parties at least speak a common language and therefore, their exchange of opinions may improve the fruit of their endeavor.

But at the end we meet a **seemingly irresolvable problem**. What happens when there is no agreement in a society on the most basic tenets of natural law? Certainly, it should be easier to build up a common agreement in things like "parents should take care of their children," "to kill and to steal are wrong," and others of this type, than to agree on how high the level of taxation should be.

But even in these issues there may be no agreement, a situation common in today's pluralistic societies. There is no fundamental agreement in Northern Ireland or in Israel about the legitimacy of the use of violence to achieve nationhood status. There was no fundamental agreement about the nature of the needed social reforms in the Liberal revolutions of the XIX Century or in the Marxist revolutions of the XX Century. There is no fundamental agreement in many prosperous countries of the Western world on the right to life of the unborn baby, as there was no agreement on the issues of slavery and minorities rights.

On those cases, the minority groups that seriously see their fundamental rights infringed could be morally right in making use of violence—as it has been the case in our days in many processes of independence from colonial powers—but only after all legal democratic means have been exhausted, in such a way that the harm that could possibly be derived is minimized, the means used are in themselves good, and the good that their actions are expected to bring about is carefully compared with the wrong they may cause.

The legal systems will never contemplate the legality of such type of actions, yet they could be just. But they will avoid them if they contemplate legal procedures to redress possible situations of injustice without the need of having recourse to violence, a consideration that seems to be meaningless for Kelsen and all legal positivists.

In the meantime, it must be granted to Kelsen his portion of truth, regardless whether he considers it to be such or not. Respect for majority rule seems to be the best system to decide on matters open to opinion; and even on those issues that affect fundamental rights of men inadequately treated by the law, a reasonable democratic system grants a period of time in which a peaceful evolution from an unjust to a just solution can take place. As for the countries whose legal systems persist on founding their social pact on sand, sooner rather than later, will have to pay for it.

Those who do not believe in truth and human nature do not learn from the past; but history is extremely educational about the cause of glory and decadence of superb political constructions. Peace is the fruit of justice, and injustice is a form of violence. But the recourse to violence should always be the last resource, only to be resorted to when the inflicted injustice is unbearable and there is no other means to re-establish justice. Because peace is a great social good.

Notes

[1] 1881-1973. Jurist and legal theorist, born in Prague. He is best known as the creator of the 'pure theory of law,' in which the science of law is required to be exclusively normative and pure.

[2] Hans Kelsen. Absolutism and Revelativism in Philosophy and Politics. Am. Pol. Scie. Rev.

[3] 1889-1976

[4] Ibid 906

[5] Hans Kelsen. *Pure Theory and Law* (1967), 40.

[6] Hans Kelsen. *Das Naturrecht in der politischen Theorie*, 148

[7] Ibid 913

[8] Ibid 913

[9] This Czech mathematics showed in 1931 that any forma logical system adequate for number theory must contain propositions not provable in that system.

7

Liberty, Freedom and the Liberties

7.1 Absence of Evidence

Kelsen and other legal positivists' concern with the creation of a legal framework within which tolerance--and tolerance alone--can reign is noble but misguided. There is no **historical evidence** that such an adventure has ever been neither seriously attempted nor approximated, **much less has been successful**.

Some people who fall ecstatic, for example, with the *tolerance* that allegedly existed among the three great monotheistic religions in mediaeval Moslem Spain, seem to ignore that when the Almohads invaded Al Andalus in the XII Century, the most outstanding citizens of Cordoba, the Moslem Averroes and the Jew Maimonides, had to flee the city.

The *tolerant* Roman Empire persecuted the Christians and razed to the ground the Temple of Jerusalem; liberal England oppressed the Irish and let them die of hunger in the time of famine; contemporary France has prohibited Moslem girls to go to school wearing a veil; after Second World War, the United States condemned the Spaniards to a decade of hunger simply because its government did not like General Franco. *Homo sum et nihil humanum alienum a me puto.*[1]

To conclude from here that tolerance is not a real asset, that there has not been progress in tolerance, and that some societies have achieved greater degree of tolerance than others would be mistaken; it only serves as a reminder that **absolute tolerance is Utopia**, as proven by the fact that even democratic America--probably the most tolerant of modern nations--upheld slavery rights until a hundred and fifty years ago and that race discrimination was an almost unchallenged social fact in the US well until our own days.

History must be read as a **permanent conflict between justice and abuse of power**; given man's existential condition as fallen and redeemed, he experiences in his heart an unceasing struggle between granting to others what is due to them and seeking self-gratification; man has a double vision of the world: one centered on himself and another centered on God, more natural and much more in agreement with the reality of things, where others have a place of reference equivalent at least to one's own place.

The paternity of the notion that **laws should protect the freedom of the citizens** belongs to the ancient Greeks, but among them such principle applied only to a privileged few and the same could be said of the Romans, the greatest legislators of all times: even if they brought to the world a substantial expansion of civil tolerance, their tolerance was elitist: in other words, tolerance for a few.

The primitiveness of the Germanic and Slavic invaders--not to mention the Huns, Arabs, etc.--brought a deep retrogression to civilization and therefore to tolerance. It was left in the hands of the Church to bring both back, through a long and not always successful task of social education.

Christianity propelled growing awareness of man's dignity seeing in him God's image and likeness, **recognizing the existence of true human rights founded in his nature**, even if the shortsightedness or crooked heart of Christians brought forth serious drawbacks. Religious intolerance has been one of those areas where Christian men and women have failed at times to recognize that no one can be discriminated for religious beliefs.

7.2 Non Causa pro Causa (Taking as cause what is not the real cause)

Not only there is no historical evidence that tolerance alone ever built peaceful societies, but common sense suffices to show that, in fact, is incapable of it. Given that the inclination to sin is present in the heart of man and that a power without moral or external constraints is prone to abuse, bringing injustice to the social body, it is obvious that **tolerance without limits is by its own nature self-destructive**. When limits are not set to the actuation of men, the strong ones tend to impose themselves upon the weak for their own benefit, as animals do. Probably the master and the model of all tyrants of modern times, Napoleon Bonaparte, was at the same time the greatest champion of the Liberal cause. He brought as much destruction as he did good because his will was law and his personal sword was the enforcer of *la Liberté*.

The ideal of a society as free and, therefore, as tolerant as possible has to be framed by laws--and enforced by the corresponding executive powers--that guarantee that the natural and original rights of all the citizens are always respected. **Absence of principle and rule of the majority are not adequate means to build a genuine social freedom**; what is needed is that the best citizens make a committed defense of the principles of justice, even when those principles go against the will of those holding *majority* of power, money, social influence, or control of the media. **The natural--not necessarily legal--rights of the individual persons and social groups are the limits to tolerance**, regardless of the opinion of the majority.

I would like to bring here a quotation that an eminent exponent of classical juridical thought issued during the granting of a doctorate *honoris causa* of another great man of Law: Law ordains according to justice the peaceful coexistence of individuals and of nations and sets guarantees against the abuses and the tyranny of those who would like to live and to govern according to their own capricious choice or their prepotent power."[2]

Classical thought always understood that the limits of tolerance are marked not only by the possible abuses of power but also by the attempts to impose lifestyles that are offensive to the *moral sensibility of the community*. One cannot go around naked on the streets or, as it is the case with a number of democratic countries, one cannot express in public opinions praising the horrible crime of the Holocaust. On the other hand, the categories of living and governing are diverse: there could be more tolerance in society about carelessly living than about power abuse, especially when the abuser represents a democratically elected majority.

7.3 Freedom and Liberté

The entry of the port of New York is graced by the **Statue of Liberty**: she has welcomed men and women running away from tyranny from all over the world; but the political freedom it symbolizes is not to be identified with that other **freedom** that is inherent to the human person. Someone has wittingly written that a parallel statue should be erected somewhere around as a reminder dedicated to **Responsibility**, because the Liberty hailed by the French revolutionaries was exclusively meant to be absence of **self attributed** and **abusive** power of governance, but not personal freedom, that is inseparable from personal responsibility.

This affirmation requires further precision since languages play tricks. The original roots of words are habitually found in the concrete, rather than in abstract notions. The English *free* seems to come from the Sanskrit, via Old German, and means *released from bondage, imprisonment, or restrain*, so it is better understood as *set free from*; the English *liberty* comes from the Latin *libertas*, an abstract noun derived from *liber* that has a connotation somehow similar to free, although *liber* has also another precise meaning: it is inseparably connected with *liberi, the children*, as opposed to *the serfs, servi.*

Even if **freedom and liberty** were taken as synonyms, it would always be possible to distinguish in them two different nuances: one of them, better derived from the Latin **liber** applies to the condition of certain human beings who *are free*; the other one makes reference to some particular situations where *men are not obliged or conditioned by something else in some aspects of their actuation*: Solzhenitsyn has described with unusual vigor the inner freedom of men working under inhuman conditions in concentration camps.

According to Aquinas, "human freedom is the property of the human will through which he determines himself in his actions towards his end." **Our essential freedom**, therefore, is not the power of doing whatever we want. We are limited and there are many things that we would like to do and yet we will not be able to do. To think that human freedom consists in doing everything we would like to is a mirage that imagines that we creatures possess something that belongs exclusively to God[3]. But we are really free because when we chose something, *we do it by ourselves* and no other power can force on us a different choice: this capacity to claim that our acts are ours is the root of our dignity and responsibility.

We easily conclude from this digression that the cry of the French bourgeois for *liberté* was directed towards some specific political freedoms that they felt had been historically usurped from them by someone else.

7.4 Magistra Vitae. A Lesson from History

The story is an old one, as old as mankind. The ancient aristocratic Roman Republic, a democracy reserved to an elite, was in shambles. **Julius Caesar** tried to bring order back to the commonwealth through an accumulation of powers in his person and was assassinated. **Augustus** succeeded making himself emperor and transforming the position into a hereditary one, but the Roman populace would not mind the change because he brought back greatness, peace and order to the nation and because in the past they, the people, had very little to say in the government of the Republic.

Leadership among the Barbarians was mostly **elective** among the chieftains; this form of democracy was extraordinarily messy, often ending in assassination and ruling by the strongest. **Christian Medieval kings had little power** and was mostly curtailed by the nobility: but they reserved to themselves the right to implement justice and so, they spent their lives waging war against unruly nobles; their position of power was made hereditary once again, a change accepted by their peoples because the order of succession by blood lineage was better than the anarchy that election brought about. Many **Renaissance monarchs** used their power for the benefit of their own greatness and that of their dynasty enlarging their states through marriages of their children; imposed themselves into their subjects as Machiavellian autocrats unifying their countries and keeping them in submission through carrot and stick. During the **Enlightenment period**, an elite of genuine patriotic aristocrats and bourgeois granted themselves totalitarian powers under the cover of the **divine right of the kings** whom they served: power, now, was not only hereditary but came straight from God, even if a good number of ancestors of the kings had been plain usurpers.

This historical panoramic view was needed in order to make clear that the cry *Liberté* meant the rejection on the part of a larger minority of the bourgeois--most of them lawyers--of the self-attributed kingly divine right to govern other men through a clique of clever fellows appointed with the finger. As it usually happens in the revolutions, the winners swept alike past rights and wrongs, abolished abusive powers but also rightful privileges, brought in anarchy and ended taking over positions similar to those previously occupied by the ousted aristocrats. Chaos offered new chances to the strongest who changed the motto of Louis XIV *I am the State[4]* into a more comprehensive *I am the State and Liberty at the same time and all the peoples of the Europe are supposed to obey me.* The new tyrant--Napoleon--abolished, in the name of Liberty, real freedoms painfully won through secular struggles by kingdoms, regions, municipalities, universities, guilds, welfare institutions, deserving individuals, as well as by the Church.

In spite of the French revolutionaries' devotion to democracy theirs, like the one of the ancient Greeks, was a democracy only for a few who enjoyed sufficient yearly income, namely themselves; and, as for tolerance, the heinous Terror of the Jacobins, shows that they did not believe too much on it.

The treasure of conquered real freedoms of the ancient world, was destroyed on the pretext of **equality under the law** –Egalité--; in reality it was destroyed because it was much easier for the winners to exercise absolute power when the natural defenses of society had been lowered down. The new elite needed power because their aim was to change not only the abuses in society, but man himself and for that purpose they needed to destroy the Church and to control the educational system: the pendulum swung back from one abuse to another.

7.5 Real Freedoms and the Power Needed to Uphold the Common Good

That **these lessons of history have a permanent value**, can be seen in a comment by Robert Harris in *The Daily Telegraph* of London of November 28th, 2001. "All governments, be they elected or imposed, strive ceaselessly to maximize their power, and never is this more easily done than during wartime. If the [British] government's proposed new powers of arrest and detention, interception and suppression are pushed through, we may take it as absolutely certain that the rights that are being taken away will never be restored. The new technologies have the potential to destroy human privacy and the government now means to exploit the situation under cover of fighting terrorism. It could be a peculiar paradox if, supposedly in defense of the supreme Western ideal of personal freedom, we allowed the creation of a society in which personal freedom was permitted only under Home Office license; yet such may be the price of *our state of perpetual alertness.*"

History teaches that **keeping authority legitimate and political power within bounds** is a great and legitimate ideal difficult to achieve, since it is threatened by those who in society hold the real powers, those who by controlling weapons, money, education and information services are capable of agitating the masses, shaping public opinion and the like.

When the existing cultural, economic and social conditions are favorable, democracy is probably the best way to achieve the lofty ideal of *Liberté*, when the conditions do not favor it, the common good seems to be more relevant to society than liberty.

Bertrand de Jouvenel has written that there are two legitimate forms of exercise of power: one of the **Rex**, *a mere presence of arbitration in a healthy society*, the other of the **Dux**, that *concentrates power on a limited number of hands in order to protect the common good in times of crisis*. The first form of exercise of power is threatened by anarchy when the conditions for democracy are not present, while tyranny maybe the outcome of the second, if extraordinary powers are kept after the emergency situation that could have justified it is over.

To avoid the risk taken by the institution of the **Dux** recognized by the Roman Republic as a solution to a crisis, the duration of his position was limited only to one year: whoever tried to last longer would be ousted; equally in ancient Greek, absolute rulers could be temporarily banished from the land--ostracized--by popular vote.

During colonial times and also after the transfer of sovereignty, Hong Kong enjoyed prosperity under a mild form of dictatorship; likewise Singapore has after independence. The Philippines, in spite of a long training in democracy cherished by the people, does not seem to find its path towards good government.

Tension between the power needed to uphold the common good, of which the real freedoms, justice, and tolerance are very important portions, and the risk that excessive power may be perpetuated is unavoidable; the purpose of the laws that the peoples give to themselves is to find adequate solutions to this problem according to their own traditions, idiosyncrasies and the historical period they live in.

Strong private institutions help to keep the balance. As Messner said, the ideal is for the *State to hold as much power as needed, while society should be as strong as possible.*

7.6 Genuine Freedom

Real freedoms vary from one nation, region, and historical period to another. Although absolutely loyal to their kings to the point of self-sacrifice, the great playwrights of Spain's imperial times. Lope de Vega and Calderon de la Barca, praised the people of the town of Fuenteovejuna and the Mayor of Zalamea for killing royal representatives who had abused authority. The people of the Basque town of Tolosa, killed the Jew Gabaon commissioned by the King, for trying to levy taxes of which they had been exempted. El Cid obliged his King to swear not to have taken part in the assassination of his brother. The nobility of Aragon accepted a newly sworn king as superior to each one of them in particular although obliged him to acknowledge that all together were more than him. Real freedoms were in the ancient world something concrete and tangible but were mostly abolished in the name of an abstract *Liberté.*

The sweeping leveling brought to Western Europe by the French revolution is now on the reverse: ancient kingdoms demand devolution; old regions their autonomy; professional bodies claim the right to be consulted in issues that affect them; private universities are taking their revenge upon those established by the State after liberal governments decided to suppress the old ones founded by the Church. The people of Puerto Rico ask the Navy to abandon a base imposed by force on their territory. And a long etc., because *the peoples of the world are much more interested in their concrete freedoms than in Liberty,* a concept too vague to mean anything real.

7.7 Respect for Personal and Institutional Freedom

Tolerance for diversity is a good thing as long as personal justice is protected and individual behavior does not offend the collective sensibilities of the established society. Although there is nothing wrong with smoking a cigarette, one *should* not do it in a circle of people who abhor the smell of tobacco; but to forbid by law smoking in all circumstances would be an act of tyranny.

Tolerance with evil that is the cause of injustice to other persons is unjust tolerance: for example, to allow abortion under the excuse that women can do with their own body whatever they want is a crime since the life of another human being is being destroyed.

Whenever reasonable and possible, liberty should be a main social goal although there could be circumstances where the common good should prevail over it. As for man's freedom, he is free by nature and everybody's freedom must be protected, guided and enhanced by laws encouraging its responsible use. The freedom of decision of voluntary groups needs to be equally protected against possible abuses on the part of the powerful and monopolistic tendencies of the State itself.

The main attacks to freedom do not come in our days so much in the form of physical violence as in the form of ideological pressure, propaganda, and misinformation. It is pitiful to see how governments of nations that brand themselves democratic and tolerant, try to trap their own citizens through campaigns aimed at shaping their behavior according to the ideological prejudices of those who are in power. It is even more pitiful to see how these same nations apply their powerful resources to twist the arms of the governments of poor and weak nations forcing them to accept their own liberal dogmas--population control, globalization--and whatever else suits their selfish interests.

It is right time for all those who love man's genuine freedom to raise their voice in defense of the freedom of those whose freedom can more easily be downtrodden; the freedom of the poor, small, and weak to do things their own way, while giving them a helping hand in following their path of material development and institutional maturity. Encouraging them to make their peoples aware of their dignity and rights while progressing in the institutional respect for human rights. Because, ultimately, history teaches that **liberties are conquered rather than granted** and that only those who really appreciate them will exert the social pressure that is needed so that those in authority accept that the time has arrived to replace the old molds by new ones, more tolerant and free and also much more just.

Notes

[1] I am a man and I do not consider myself beyond anything human (Cicero).

[2] Josemaria Escrivá. Quoted by J. Echevarria: Memoria del Beato Josemariá, page 148. Ed Rialp. Madrid, 2000

[3] J. de Torre. *Christians Philosophy,* Manila

[4] L'Etat c'est moi. (Before the Parlement de Paris , 13 April165)

8

Legal Tolerance and Respect for Personal Convictions

8.1 Polemic Aftermath to September 11, 2001

The terrorist attack recently suffered by the United States has offered to the world press an opportunity to release rivers of murky waters, renewing *old tirades against religion on the pretext of defending social tolerance.* An article of the recent Nobel Price winner of Literature and avowed Communist Party member, José Samarago, takes the extreme position. Writing in *La Repubblica[1],* he made an arrogant manifestation of atheism. "I have already said that all religions, all without exception, will never be of any use in bringing men together and reconciling them but, on the contrary, they have been and still continue being the cause of much unspeakable suffering, ravages and physical and spiritual violence, constituting some of the darkest episodes of man's history." Regardless of the professed faith, he attributes to the idea of God the guilt for the darkest human tragedies; in the context of Samarago's life, is not risky to guess that religion means in fact Christianity.

A few days later Vittorio Messori answered him in the *Corriere della Sera***[2]** saying that the first serious attempt to eliminate Christianity and to create a "rational form of worship, " took place during the French Revolution: in two years, 1792-3, the Revolution made 40, 000 victims, 84 per cent of which belonged not to the nobility but to the Third State (farmers, small bourgeois, etc.); to which has to be added the genocide of La Vendee programmed and implemented by the Jacobins, that killed 34% of the population of the region, 120,000 faithful Catholics. In more recent times those techniques already explored by the Jacobins were perfected by Marxist regimes, that killed more than 100 million persons; (...) in the East, the attempt to proclaim the death of God, brought forth men's death."

A century and a half ago, Marxist thought had already described religion as the *opiate of the people*, destined to disappear either violently, a method favored by the classical *praxis*, or simply by consumption, nowadays a more popular opinion. According to the *South China Morning Post* of 13-XII-2001, President Jiang Zemin reminded the attendants to a conference finished the day before that Communist Party members "must stand firm on their atheist principles" although "we must recognize the fact that religions will exist under socialism for a long time. What has to be done is to ask religious believers to embrace our socialist system, the leadership of the Communist Party..., etc. " And he added resolutely, "what we will not tolerate is any attempts to jeopardize national and ethnic unity under pretext of religion." In other words, religious **beliefs** could be allowed to go on for a while, as long the socialist system and the leadership of the Communist Party are held as **dogmas**.

8.2 Liberal Thought

Opposite to Marxism stands Liberalism, perhaps the most influential ideology of modern age, "a broad cultural movement which defies accurate analysis and whose history deserves careful study."[3] Certainly it does, since many notions enclosed in the term *liberal* (generous, open minded, tolerant, free from prejudice) are dear to most men while others are at least confused.

As a system of thought, Liberalism has a program in mind. According to the Webster's Dictionary it is "a political or social philosophy advocating the freedom of the individual, parliamentary systems of government, non-violent modification of political social economic institutions to assure unrestricted development in all spheres of human endeavor and governmental guarantees of individual rights and civil liberties, " all of them praise-deserving objectives.

However, the term carries other shades of meaning which are open to question. Many serious intellectuals think that behind its lofty ideals. Liberalism tends to place the individual above the common good, neglects social justice and human solidarity and is always at risk of landing in a kind of pleasure-condoning and permissiveness-seeking egoism. The objection is so grave that a group of honest modern Liberals are striving hard to reconcile those community values with their liberal tradition.

To which has to be added the inaccuracy of claiming that historical Liberalism has not advocated violent modifications of the institutions, because the rationalization for the most furious social conflicts of the past two centuries was the need of implanting in society the liberal ideals: the Jacobin Terror, the wars of conquest of Napoleon and the Continental liberal revolutions around 1830 , 1845 and 1860, etc., all used violent means.

Most popular among them was in Spain the one commanded around 1830 by a military officer, a certain Riego. It was complete, including its own hymn whose lyrics the wit of the people of Madrid changed in the music halls:

La libertad del mundo
proclamo en aha voz
y muera el que no piense
igual que pienso yo!

(Aloud I proclaim the freedom of the world; death to those who do not think like me!)

Liberal governments of the Western countries made also use of violence to build up civilizing empires and former colonies resorted likewise to terrorism or overt action to gain freedom from oppressive imperial rule: the assumption that Liberalism advocates not violent change was obviously made by a Liberal sympathizer, not by a historian.

Liberalism is an ideological chameleon ephemeral in content and in permanent state of flow. In the last three decades it has even developed great affinity for contemporary Socialism which on the other hand has renounced to its central ideas of controlled economy managed by the State: now. Liberals and Socialists together care for lost causes like ecology, minorities and marginalised people.

Influential factions within Liberalism have maintained all throughout its history a couple of fixed reference points: the need to dismantle sexual and family ethics of the traditional Christian family and to eliminate the influence of organized religions in social life and in the legal system of the nations in particular although, of course, granting them the right to exist.

Peguy already noted that "the root issues behind the evolution of ideologies are theological and philosophical questions such as happiness, after-life, freedom, salvation, truth, peace." The reason for the conflicting attitudes found in Liberalism is that, beyond its passionate defense of so many legitimate personal and social freedoms, it evolved into an ideology with its radicalism, prejudices and biases, pretending to be a holistic solution to all problems of mankind, while in fact, leaving unsolved most of the fundamental human issues.

8.3 Ideologies can Become Threats to Social Tolerance

When a radical group of intellectuals claims the monopoly of know-how of the path that will lead to the establishment a peaceful, happy and an everlasting **new world order**, mankind can expect trouble; more often than not, they will reason out that using violence is an unpleasant but unavoidable step to the successful implementation of the new Utopia.

Violence can be *physical,* like imperial conquest, liberation war, guerrilla or terrorism; the latest was invented towards the end of the XIX Century in Latin and Slavonic countries as the ultimate Anarchist weapon and has passed through dormant and active periods all the way to the tragic events of September 11.

But there is another form of violence of *psychological nature called social engineering,* more subtle albeit no less threatening, that consists in applying cultural economic, educational or legal pressure to the citizenry to oblige them to accept progressive social changes whose sole justification is found in the ideological whims of the group in power.

Occurrences of this type of violence are manifest and frequent: governments of rich nations considering that population growth in poor countries is a threat to the stability of their own welfare, force them to sign population control agreements reached at properly orchestrated international conferences: unless they do so, not only their international respectability will suffer but they will be deprived of much needed developmental grants; democratic governments impose on the educational system of the nation tax financed programs loaded with ideological content; Supreme Courts composed of a few appointed wise men of law, conclude to be unable to decide if a fetus is or is not subject to legal rights, especially to the one to life, source of all other rights and after such declaration of ignorance, impose on the Social Security system of their countries the obligation to finance abortions; etc. Examples of this sort could be multiplied to infinity, with the aggravating factor that those legal and administrative acts of violence from the top are enhanced by the help of powerful media campaigns.

The skeptics of the efficacy of psychological violence will do well reading the works of the Marxist reformer Antonio Gramsci[4], urging the destruction of the Christian values of the people as a requirement previous to implanting Communism through campaigns of promotion of bourgeois counter-values like pornography and financial corruption serving as Trojan horse of the revolution; counter-values that on due time will be uprooted to give way to a renewed Marxist Puritanism.

8.4 Religions and Ideologies

Religions differ from ideologies because, unlike them, they do not constitute close intra-mundane holistic systems; religions look outside man and the world for the ultimate cause of all things, to a transcendent reality called God. Some of them are the fruit of the effort of the human spirit seeking Him, others claiming to be depositaries of His self-manifestation. Religion establishes a **religa-**

tio, a profound relationship *between man and God.* Since God is the Supreme reality, religions ordinarily encompass some form of personal and public worship and codes of personal and collective ethical behavior that bind men in the depth of their spirit, in their conscience.

Earlier we arrived at the conclusion that legal systems must guarantee to individuals and groups *as much freedom as possible, while protecting the demands of justice,* without which social peace it is not possible. Now, it is undeniable that the world religions have configured the culture of the nations where they prevailed, not only offering their own peculiar appreciation of the world and of human realities, but also structuring society and enhancing unique aesthetic feelings; none of these features ever threatened justice or social harmony but, on the contrary, made outstanding contributions to the ethical and cultural enrichment of the peoples. Accordingly, it belongs to the essence of any legal system to ensure *religious freedom to the nation's citizens.*

In the course of history organized societies marked by strong ethnic, cultural and religious identity, felt often endangered by unjust external attacks and fought legitimately for self-defense, *pro patria et altare*; but there have been cases too when some men have applied physical or moral coercion upon legitimate, independent forms of behavior of persons or minorities living in their midst on the name of the dominant religion, that then degenerated into a dangerous form of ideology: civil society has the right and the duty of stopping those expansionist attempts in defense of the religious freedom of the citizens.

In the ideologies, like in the religions, valid truths may coexist with blatant errors. In fact, ideologies came out as the result of the secularization of the world order, attempting to occupy the space left empty by the religions they had displaced, inventing their own forms of civil worship and building up lay moral systems of their own, including intra-mundane sanctions and rewards: Compte's Positivism or Marxism are outstanding examples.

Man's fundamental moral duty is to seek the ultimate truth of his existence following the dictates of his conscience; therefore, no moral or religious obligation can be imposed on him through any form of physical, psychological or legal coercion. The legal systems of the nations are called to guarantee public *religious and ideological tolerance,* as long as the fundamental demands of justice and the common good are satisfied.

8.5 The Genuine Meaning of Juridical Tolerance

Precision is imperative when speaking about ultimate concepts. Tolerances described in the Webster's Dictionary as "fair, objective and permissive attitude towards those, whose opinions practices, race, religion, nationality etc differ from one's own." But in a related sense of the term it is also used to refer to a "liberal, undogmatic view point." There is a third significance to it as "allowing the right of something that one does not approve," and a fourth that implies "the allowance of conduct with which one is not in accord." There are important differences of meaning among these four different usages of the term.

· First of all, there is little in common between opinions, practices and religion on one hand and race and nationality on the other; permissive attitude towards different nationalities or races can only mean patronizing them since people of other races or nationalities are not supposed to be *permitted* but must be *recognized and respected* for their intrinsic human dignity.

· The second meaning given to *tolerance* as "liberal, undogmatic point of view" seems to be a description viewed from the perspective of Liberalism. To the classical Latin, the word **dogma** meant "philosophical doctrine," from which the Catholic Church derived the meaning of "a truth formally revealed by God which has been proposed by the teaching authority of the Church to be believed as suc." The English language has added other connotations, because the adjective undogmatic can mean not only *unproposed* by the Church as a formally revealed truth--its proper Christian meaning--but also "asserting *opinions* in doctrinaire or arrogant manner."

The Dictionary's suggestion that opinions must be presented as opinions, not as truths, is correct but it would be unlawful to conclude that to present truth as truth (example: two plus two equals four) means lack of tolerance and is therefore, *unliberal* unless, of course, someone is of the *opinion that truth is not attainable and so any categorical statement is socially disturbing,* in whose case his own statement would have been a mere opinion. Now, this attitude is not infrequent among Liberal doctrinaires who can behave as dangerous ideologists because of their radicalism and aggressiveness.

· The next meaning of *tolerance* as to allow "*the right* of something that one does not approve," implying that a person tolerates in others something only in so far as it is their *real right,* disregarding his own likes of dislikes. I think that more than tolerance this is *plain sense of justice,* as long as we consider that the right is not merely legal but a real one, because no one can have a real right to do wrong. If the term *right* refers to a *legal right to do something immoral,* the term tolerance would acquire ambiguous shades because, as the next meaning of tolerance suggests, one can allow certain wrong to go on unpunished but in no way consider it a legitimate right: that would be a transvestite of justice.

· Finally, *tolerance* as "the allowance of conduct with which one is not in accord," is the *classical meaning of the term describing the noble attitude of someone who thinks that some forms of behavior are morally wrong yet should be allowed to go without being openly opposed or punished.* This kind of tolerance that has nothing to do with an agnostic attitude in relation to the capacity of man to reach certainties in the moral and religious orders, but derives from the need of harmonizing civil and religious societies in order not to jeopardize the common good. As for the tolerance with religious error we have already said that no one should suffer coercion because of his beliefs, since the human intelligence surrenders only to truth, but humans easily take error for truth.

When saying that the legal system must be the guarantor of religious and ideological tolerance two things are affirmed: that one of its most important missions is to make sure that no one, neither government, nor religious or ideological pressure groups is allowed to impose arbitrary opinions or ideological postulates on individual citizens or groups by means of physical, legal or psychological pressure; and that some form of immoral behavior may often be left unsanctioned--not fostered nor encouraged--for the sake of social peace and harmony, both important ingredients of the common good. One of the primordial objectives of any legal system is to try to achieve as much social freedom as possible.

The fundamental laws of every State and its higher organs of legal interpretation are burdened with the tremendous responsibility of guaranteeing freedom from coercion: especially that coercion that may be exercised by the executive powers, the political parties and other social groups possessing excessive coercive or economic power or disproportionate control of the mass media.

8.6 Legislative and Judiciary Systems as Promoters of Values

Although justice is often uncertain, the laws must procure it with determination because no social peace is possible without it; but to seek justice is not the only mission entrusted to the law-making and applying bodies.

A substantial segment of their mission is to foster and protect universally accepted human values: respect for human dignity, understanding, forgiveness, openness to strangers, solidarity, generosity, communication of intellectual, moral and material goods among persons and nations, desires of making others happy. These are values shared by billions of the best and most noble human beings.

Many of them have been Christian gifts to the Western world but are similarly found in other world religions and are greatly appreciated by the best men even in secularized societies because of their humanizing influence; a somber feature of the present culture is a number of self-seeking prestigious individuals who, blinded by ambition and ferocious individualism and driven by the search for immediate gratification, despise and try to ignore those noble values that have been handed to us; under pretext of tolerance and agnosticism they foster libertine attitudes that tantamount to retrogression to animal behavior.

No wonder that the counterfeit values prevalent in the many Western nations are opposed by many other peoples of the world otherwise eager to assimilate many of the West's positive achievements. Christian tradition has been disavowed by its rightful heirs who offer to the rest of mankind awful examples of selfish and rapacious behavior, while proclaiming their right to judge and chastise them: their conduct, as harmful to themselves as to those who never possessed before that wonderful heritage, it is a somber presage of future conflicts.

Notes

[1] 20-IX-2001

[2] 14-X-2001

[3] J. de Torre. Contemporary Philosophical Issues in Historical Perspective.

[4] 1891-1937. A founder of the Italian Communist Party.

9

International Order: Rights of the Nations and the Rights of Man

9.1 A Historical Review

It is not difficult to perceive all throughout Western history a permanent underlying effort to build more just societies inspired in Christian principles of solidarity, with the help of law.

The legislative corpus of those Christian kingdoms was for centuries traditional, simple and stable, features that contributed to make it venerable and commonly accepted. The motto of the Basque Nationalist Party that, like many others similar political movements of the XIX Century aimed at the independence of its own people inspired in the current romantic fad of one people-one state, was God and Ancient Laws (***Jangoikoa eta Lege sarrá***): a veritable relic of old mediaeval Europe.

In those ancient times too, conflicts between nobility and people, kings and nobles and among kings themselves were not infrequent and every now and then the accumulation of judiciary and executive powers in the hands of the monarchs made them prone to abuse and arbitrary administration of justice. Matters worsened when princes of the Renaissance, strongly inclined to impose their own will, ignored the rights of the traditional representative bodies. Parliaments, *Cortes*, Diets and the like, threatening or manipulating them: a good example being Henry VIII's Supremacy Act, where the fate of Christianity in England became subordinated to the Royal sexual whims. The Enlightened Despots, present all over Europe, went even further: "I am the State," the French monarch proclaimed; while the Austrian Emperor enjoyed himself regulating the schedules of Masses in the Churches of the Empire: even in our days examples of that sort are not infrequent.

Montesquieu's proposal of dispersing the different powers to avoid their accumulation in one or a few hands, was quite timely and thanks to him today's secularized nations enjoy more effective guarantees against abuses than ever in the past.

The reform of the distribution of political power took place within the boundaries of national states; but, what was the situation in the global world? Today like in old times, beyond compromise among conflicting parties, there are only three available solutions to solve or avoid conflicts: empire, arbitrage, and war. Empires, even if animated by the best intentions, have often been arbitrary and supremacist; arbitrage seldom worked; and war was always cruel, resulting, more often than not, in situations having little to do with genuine justice.

It was the glory of the creators of the *Jus Gentium* to have concluded the *necessity of an international law,* founded in that set of universally acceptable principles of social ethics known as *natural law.* Not that both things coincided, as Francisco Suarez explained in 1612[1], since the *Ius Gentium,* although based on the realities of the human nature, remained a product of the human will and was therefore, a law of human origin. Within the framework of a Christian Empire, the Law of the nations was a good instrument to try to establish justice and, as a result, peace.

Reading *De Indiis* (1538) of the remarkable Francisco de Vitoria, father of the *Jus Gentium,* is a moving experience. The author, a Dominican friar, questioned the legal capacity of the Pope to allot kingdoms since he was not the temporal sovereign of the world. He considered the *Indios*--the native Americans--to be members of the international community and their groupings, tribes, villages, etc., sovereign states.

Vitoria was a real forerunner of globalization who thought that natural ports should be open for everyone to trade and that outsiders should be allowed to settle there as long as they did not cause harm to the land; that foreign trade and commerce was a human right that only ceased to be one when the common good of the states was at the stake. Therefore, within the framework of a Christian Empire justice for less developed peoples was still an attainable ideal as long as the principles of the *Jus Gentium* were kept.

With the Enlightenment, Western society that at that time was already only nominally Christian, became so secularized that the international order experienced a regression towards the Law of the Jungle. The only available mechanism for peace was the *balance of power.* As long as the Great Powers were quiet and even, a temporary peace was still possible, out of fear more than out of conviction, but the periodical breaches of that unstable equilibrium brought rivers of blood to XIX and XX Century Europe.

In Second World War and in the never fought Cold War, balance of power went on together with ideological struggle, both adversaries seeking global supremacy. Thank God Freedom won, offering a unique chance to build a *new world order based on justice and peace.*

9.2 Sovereignty

As a fruit of the liberal revolutions of the XIX Century, the abstract notion of *sovereignty* as a *supreme and independent power and authority* in government possessed or claimed by a state or community, occupied the place of the absolute monarchies of old. The notion of absolute sovereignty, lacking internal consistency is today intellectually discredited, but those who actually control big junks of world power do not seem to be particularly eager to share it with others.

As we saw at the beginning of this series the ontological reason for the existence of juridically organized societies is the personal decision to surrender to others legally constituted in authority a portion of one's own power for the sake of achieving certain common goods.

It seems beyond discussion that a number of individuals could first decide to renounce a portion of their personal autonomy to a certain social group and then another portion to a higher level group, with the condition that the previous decision is respected. Privilege (private law) is as much law as general law is, and privilege rights can only be lost by gracious voluntary transfer: any violation of the social pact invoking sovereign rights constitutes plain tyrannical usurpation.

National groups endowed with common ethnic or cultural features have a natural right to independence as long as they constitute a large majority within a territory, although such right can be partially or totally transferred to a larger grouping; but there is no reason why that cession cannot be recalled, especially when future generations of that nation feel maltreated by the hegemonic power: this recalling is called in present parlance *devolution.*

Not to accept this principle would be equivalent to deny the right of independence to Ireland, Korea, Poland, Singapore, Denmark, the Philippines or Israel and it is not easy to see what the difference could be between the situation of the populations of those nations when they got their independence and the one of the Basques, Scots, Tibetans, Portoricans or Taiwanese.

This statement is not intended to mean that those peoples should aim at being independent nations: as long as they enjoy sufficient autonomy to guarantee their cultural identity and their cherished privileges, including well-defined legislative privileges, quite often union within a larger group is more enriching and contributing to the common good.

The issue at stake is to make clear that within limits, such decision concerns the peoples themselves and not strangers. Impositions like the ones made by the Allies in the treaty of Versailles of dismantling the Austro-Hungarian Empire, the creation of Czechoslovakia, where Bohemians and Moravians controlled de facto the Sudetenland and Slovakia; the one of Yugoslavia where old culturally-conscious nations like Slovenia and Croatia were handled over to the Serbians; the one of giving the Saarland to France and Danzig to Poland, all of them were arbitrary manifestations of abuse of power on the part of the then winning Empires which, other considerations aside, offered some good reasons for a German revenge. When decisions like these are made for geopolitical reasons by powerful outsiders we can properly speak of *imperialism*: from the Latin *imperium*, a command.

On the other side of the spectrum, globalization entails giving up or sharing certain powers previously considered as sovereign. The best contemporary example is the European Union where a number of previously sovereign nations have agreed to cede some of their decision powers in favor of supranational authorities with the purpose of achieving obvious greater goods. The World Trade Organization, Asean, Mercosur are further examples of the same participated sovereignty. Globalization seemingly unstoppable, the notion of sovereignty itself has become obsolete, offering possibilities for a new world order hitherto unthinkable.

9.3 Rethinking the Foundations of Juridical Order

The reality of globalization will demand the development of a new word juridical system. I was talking to a good friend of mine, a lawyer of the Air Forces of my country, when we got the news that the Russians had placed the Sputnik in orbit: he soberly commented that since there were objects in space, a space law had to be created.

The much needed world juridical system cannot be any like the old international law, lacking a capacity to sanction those who broke it; much less can it be partial in favor of the powerful--remember veto power in the United Nations--or a weapon in the hands of a few nations to impose their own cultural values, no matter how legitimate, while defending their national interests.

As a result of the end of the Cold War these temptations are at present very strong. To face the real danger of Communism the free nations needed to accept unconditionally the leadership of the United States of America. A confrontation between two empires was going on in the international arena and, like the old Romans who accepted the institution of Dictatorship in times of crisis for only one year, the free world accepted for good reasons the dictatorship of the United States for a much longer period disregarding the anti-imperialistic feeling of the times. It is no easy to overcome the messianic syndrome and for a country aware of being the most powerful in the world and accustomed to command, devolution of power to where it belongs is a difficult act of self-surrender that must, on the other hand go through before a real new order can be established.

The metaphysical and ethical foundations of law, the dignity of the individual person and the need of an ordination of reason for the common good, must serve as foundations of any new world law order since the permanent disposition to give others what belongs to them, the ***suum quique,*** applies to nations or any other voluntary groupings as it does to individual persons.

9.4 Requirements of a Juridical World Order

· No real-world order can ever exist without a world **consensus on fundamental principles** of justice in international relations. They have to be few, simple, universal, permanent and binding; based on natural law, that as we saw, is only a right understanding of what persons are and how relations among them should be. Such agreement cannot be imposed, it needs to be arrived at as a free accord: must come from real consensus, not simple compromise.

Although it is not clear that such cornerstone of a new world juridical construction can ever be located in place, there are good reasons for optimism. Its content would be much less than the one of the national Constitutions, although destined to have more lasting and profound effects than them. Philosophers, jurists, sociologists and theologians, representing different nations of the planet, cultural areas and religious convictions, working patiently for as long as needed in dialogue with the peoples of the world could end up producing reasonable proposals. The ongoing conversations on Christian Ecumenism could serve as a good model of patient progress.

The greatest risk to face would be the expectable attempts on the part of those who are politically powerful to condition the result of the discussions to their political interests; even more, the foreseeable efforts of those with cultural sophistication or power of the media to try to impose their own ideological prejudices on the outcome, claiming the right to that kind of freedom of opinion that would be, once again, the freedom of the powerful to impose themselves on others.

Whatever is a fundamental right of man at the personal level is the source of any other right and can never be overshadowed by national interests or global considerations. Nothing within this world consensus should carry not even the slightest ideological undertones: just to mention a few, matters like population control, social equality or ecological concerns or even one man-one-vote political representation, regardless their importance, should be totally excluded since they either could be worked out at national level or be object of multilateral agreements.

· Once a consensus achieved, world legislative, judiciary and **executive authorities** will be needed, without which no juridical order would be possible; in their absence, the place of law will immediately be taken over by the Darwinian principle of the survival of the fittest.

By voluntary agreement these world authorities should be entrusted with *ultimate residual but fundamental sovereignty.* Within the context of the classical but mistaken notion of sovereignty this way of speaking seems almost contradictory, but it is not within a real understanding of what the term entails. In a global society sovereignty needs to be utterly dispersed; to cede different portions of one's own power in a limited and controlled manner to different legitimately authorities, according to the nature of diverse common goods is a requirement of the ultimate common good of social freedom; otherwise, Leviathan may engulf and devour us.

Therefore, a world order requires ultimate autonomy of blocks and of national, regional or professional groupings; in other words, an absolute respect for privileges, that is to say for *private laws.* There is an urgent need to redress the mistaken notion expounded by liberal rationalist thought--French Revolutionists and Socialist ideologists--that privilege is an obstacle to equality in front of the law: in fact it is the only defense against totalitarianism.

· Such a world authority should be primarily and **almost exclusively judiciary** like the best royal authority in Christian Middle Ages, since its main role would be to pass judgment in conflicting international situations declaring the *right or wrong in them according to justice.*

Its main purpose would be to prevent conflict through arbitration according to the spirit of the fundamental laws, but there will be occasions when appeal to an executive authority capable of imposing peace among conflicting parties will be needed; and also to pass judgment upon those individuals who may have committed crimes against mankind.

The corresponding executive authority must be small but efficient, truly international and independent from the national armies. For such an executive authority to be effective, military pacts among nations should be banned and no national army should be allowed to be stronger than the international force; the allowed defense budgets of individual nations should be purely defensive, limited to a small portion of their gross domestic product and submitted to international auditing. At the same time, strict international control should be established upon the international force to prevent that it could ever be used as an instrument of evil.

9.5 And Forgiveness

Ortega y Gasset wrote in the first half of the XX Century a phrase, "I am myself and my circumstances," that was much celebrated at his times although there was little on it that had not been said many times before him. Because man cannot be fully understood unless his existential condition is taken into consideration. And man is prone to do wrong, not to respect the proper ordination of justice.

A permanent lesson of history is that strict application of *objective criteria of justice* especially in the field of international grievances, has often deteriorated into revenge. In order to arise the enthusiasm of the nation and ready her for the sacrifice of war, the propaganda machinery feels entitled to present the national opponents as the epitome of evil, ignoring the warning of the Lord : "Let him who is without sin among you be the first to cast a stone at her."[2]

In a remarkable article recently written by Michael Novak for the *Asian Wall Street Journal*[3] he quotes Reinhold Niebuhr: "The problem of history is the persistent power of evil over good, even through corrupting the good. America's founders taught by the dour Saint Augustine who saw in all worldly systems the inner conflicts of injustice, never expected a pure triumph of the good. That is why they designed a system whose complicated inner struts are built on checks and balances."

And he continues warning about the dangers of the present situation. "The word 'evil' when used only of others can intoxicate the user before he knows it. I commend to him and all of us, Niebuhr's pregnant warning: **The final enigma of history is therefore not how righteous will win victory over unrighteous, but how the evil in every good and the unrighteousness of the righteous is to be overcome."**

The solution to the riddle of the sphinx has a Christian name, but one that all good people in the world can understand: **forgiveness.** In international relations, when peoples carried away by the memories of perceived past unjust treatment let themselves go and find redress in violence, often led by neurotic evil doers, they must be stopped. Those directly responsible for the unjust evil caused to others will have to suffer just punishment: but, on the whole, the misbehaving nations should also experience the embrace of forgiveness and reconciliation. As John Paul II wrote with occasion of the World Day of Prayer for Peace of 2002, "without justice there is no peace, but there can be no justice without forgiveness."

Collective defamation has often been used by the leaders of nations--with the help of wisely controlled media--as a justification of their unfair behavior in front of their own people and in order to project an international image of uprightness: trying to blackmail other peoples, perpetuating memories of past or recent evils and fostering in them a sense of historical guilt in order to keep them under subjugation is a constant incitement to revenge, the greatest possible threat against world peace and justice.

Notes

[1] Tractatus de legibus ac Deo legislatore

[2] John 8,7

[3] Michael Novak. *The return if 'Good' and 'Evil'*, The Asian Wall Street Journal, 8-II-2002

Acknowledgement

The publisher would like to gratefully acknowledge the help from the people whose work be it transcribing, proof-reading has brought this publication into reality.

About the author

Fr. Javier de Pedro was born in Tolosa, Spain in 1929. He worked as an industrial engineer for ten years. He was ordained a priest of the Prelature of Opus Dei in 1964. Soon after his ordination, he went to Philippines and in 1981 he came to Hong Kong. He remained in Hong Kong until 2013 when he returned to Philippines and has exercised his priestly activity in Manila.

www.ingramcontent.com/pod-product-compliance
Ingram Content Group UK Ltd.
Pitfield, Milton Keynes, MK11 3LW, UK
UKHW022006190726
13853UKWH00004B/1768